The Teacher's Computer Book

40 Student Projects
to Use with
Your Classroom Software

PATRICIA MOSER SHILLINGBURG
with
Kenneth Craig Bareford, Joyce Ann Paciga, and Janis Lubawsky Townsend

Teachers College, Columbia University
New York and London

Published by Teacher's College Press, 1234 Amsterdam Avenue, New York, NY 10027

Library of Congress Cataloging-in-Publication Data

Shillingburg, Patricia M.
  The teacher's computer book.

  (Computers and education series)
  1. Computer-assisted instruction. 2. Electronic
data processing. I. Title. II. Series.
LB1028.5.S485   1987   371.3'9445   86-30130

ISBN 0-8077-2824-1

Manufactured in the United States of America

92 91 90 89 88 87   1 2 3 4 5 6

Contents

Preface

The Revolution of the 1980s

When microcomputers were first introduced into the educational environment in the first half of the 1980s, the emphasis was almost totally on teaching programming in the BASIC language. There was concern that children deprived of this opportunity would be functionally illiterate in less than ten years. However, at the same time that boards of education were investing thousands of dollars in computers and teams of teachers were developing curricula, computer manufacturers were turning their attention to the creation of microcomputers with new logic systems, new vocabularies, and new software that required no knowledge of computer programming to operate. Two powerful forces were pulling in opposite directions: one to create a society of programmers; the other to create machines that required no programming skills. As in a game of tug-of-war, the rope broke in the mid-1980s.

Some of the teachers who had developed curricula for their school systems and had been teaching on computers for several years were coming to rather disturbing conclusions: Many children were not enthusiastic BASIC programmers, nor did LOGO excite them. Some children quickly raced ahead of their teachers by learning machine language and Pascal. But they were the exceptions. Many children were left behind, uninterested and, often, turned off by computers.

Many adults were also turned off by computers. They were afraid of them, confused by the jargon, suspicious that they needed a strong math background to use them, and fearful that one touch would break the machine.

However, many businessmen and businesswomen were using micro-computers. Applications in the business and academic worlds had developed along a number of well-defined lines: wordprocessing, data base management, spreadsheets, graphics, communications, and computer-assisted instruction (CAI). Programs such as Lotus 1-2-3 (with spreadsheet, data base, and graphing capabilities) combined a number of such applications. Within 18 months of Lotus's introduction, Symphony, by the same manufacturer, added wordprocessing and communications--thus combining all of the major applications in one micro-computer program. Ashton Tate had developed Framework, another powerful integrated system. Soon IBM introduced TopView, which allowed a number of independent programs to run simultaneously and to be integrated together.

At the same time that some program developers were creating expensive and complex business applications, others were writing similar and cheaper programs that performed the same tasks on computers such as the Apple II+, the Apple//e, the

IBM PCjr, the Atari, and the Commodore 64. Bank Street Writer allowed children to experience the advantages of wordprocessing; PFS File and PFS Report brought data base management to small computers in a friendly and comprehensive manner. The original VisiCalc spreadsheet program remains a standard. There are now many possibilities for graphing and graphics. And communications has opened up many new avenues of adventure for children.

Even if children need not learn BASIC or LOGO in order to be functionally literate in the adult world, they will benefit from computers in the classroom. In many schools in the country, the major acquisitions of computer hardware are completed and the computers are in place. With proportionately few additional dollars, the computers now in the schools could be used by students in the same way that they are used in the business and academic worlds: for wordprocessing, data base management, spreadsheets, graphing, and communications.

Although it is clear that most children will not need to be programmers to be computer literate as adults, we think there will continue to be considerable value in learning computer programming languages. We have watched the pure joy on the faces of many children, especially very young children, as the turtle races across the screen or crawls along the floor. It is obvious that understanding math logic and structure is reinforced by developing programming skills. And as educators, we realize that the children who will be computer scientists in the future will benefit from being exposed to programming at a young age.

A working knowledge of BASIC or LOGO is no longer requisite to being computer literate in the adult world. Knowing how to use a computer is. Just as rapidly as the technology develops, teachers must seek new strategies and new directions for teaching students to use school computers productively. Computers are here to stay. It's time to turn our attention to teaching children to use them as they are meant to be used: as tools.

This is merely the beginning.

Introduction

Using This Book

The Teacher's Computer Book is written for teachers and students to help them make practical use of the computers in their classroom. It recognizes that although a knowledge of BASIC is still useful to students, it is not a necessary skill for business or practical uses.

HARDWARE AND SOFTWARE REQUIREMENTS

Hardware

This book requires a computer with a monitor and one disk drive. In order to make the fullest use of this book, a second disk drive, a printer with graphics capability, and a Koala Pad, a modem, and a color monitor are recommended.

Because most school systems have Apples, this book is written primarily for Apple computers. However, all of the project ideas, except those that are Apple specific (primarily some in Chapter 6, "Art and Music"), are usable with most other school computers, such as the IBM PCjr, Commodore Pet, Commodore 64, TI, Atari, and TRS-80. Programs may be different from the ones we name, but similar ones--programs that do the same thing--usually exist.

Software

The following software programs are suggested: Bank Street Writer, PFS File and PFS Report, FlashCalc, PFS Graph, and ByteMaster BBS. Any similar programs--a wordprocessor, data base management program, spreadsheet, or graphing program--can be substituted.

If you are using IBM equipment, all of the software listed above is available for both the PC and the PCjr except for FlashCalc. We recommend VisiCalc if you have it or one of the spreadsheets presently being marketed for less than $100. Appendix A describes how to use the IBM Disk Operating System, and Appendix B offers an introduction to IBM BASIC.

Subscriptions to The Source and/or CompuServe are suggested.

THE ORGANIZATION OF THIS BOOK

Chapter 1 gives suggestions on how physically to set up the computer in the classroom, how to schedule its use, and when and how to use student aides.

Program disks and data disks are explained, and instructions are given on how to initialize and copy disks.

Chapters 2 through 7 contain the projects. Each chapter is on a specific application--wordprocessing, data base management, spreadsheets, graphing, art and music, and communications. These chapters begin with an outline of the goals, objectives for achieving those goals, and a list of the projects. Next there is a discussion of the application being introduced: then the projects follow. Each chapter stands by itself, so if you have Bank Street Writer but not PFS File and PFS Report, the wordprocessing chapter is independently useful.

Chapter 8 describes how computers are already affecting everyday institutions that we take for granted. Appendix A explains how to prepare to use this book with the IBM PC and the IBM PCjr. Appendix B describes drawing pictures and making music using BASIC on IBM microcomputers. Appendix C provides addresses and phone numbers for the software described in this book.

The Projects

Check the information at the top of the first page of each project. It describes what hardware and software is required to complete the project. It is assumed that each Apple computer has at least one disk drive and a monitor.

Project 1 in each chapter usually includes step-by-step instructions on how to use the suggested program. These include Bank Street Writer, PFS File and PFS Report, FlashCalc, and PFS Graph. These instructions do not, however, cover everything about the program. It is expected that teachers will learn the more complex operations and functions from the manuals that come with each program.

The rest of the projects rely on teachers and students knowing the application program. This is particularly true in wordprocessing, data base management, spreadsheets, and graphing.

The chapters on art and music and communications introduce new computer applications in each project. One of the projects in "Art and Music" uses the Koala Pad. "Communications" relies on a modem, a BBS (Bulletin Board System), and subscriptions to The Source and/or CompuServe.

It is suggested that within each chapter you proceed sequentially. That is, in "Data Base Management," play with Project 1, then do Project 2, and then 3 and 4, and then 5. If certain projects do not fit into your curriculum plan, that is not a problem--just make sure you understand any new material introduced in projects you choose not to use.

As an idea was developed for this book, other ideas for using the same techniques came to mind. You will find these additional activities at the end of many of the projects.

FINAL NOTES

Although the authors have attempted to stay up-to-date with the software, users of this book must recognize that from month to month software publishers change and improve their software. Therefore, keystroke-by-keystroke instructions may not conform with the version of software that you have. Please recognize that there may be differences.

The Teacher's Computer Book is copyrighted; you may not duplicate this book. However, for classroom purposes a teacher may copy individual projects for student use.

Having a computer in the classroom adds an exciting new dimension. It has relevance to almost everything that you are teaching--from math and English to science and social studies, from current events and good manners to organizational skills and responsibility. Before long, you will wonder how you ever taught without one.

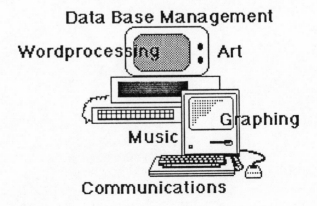

The Teacher's Computer Book

40 Student Projects to Use with Your Classroom Software

Chapter 1
Organizing for Computers

PLACING COMPUTERS IN THE CLASSROOM

Most teachers start off with one computer in their classroom. The first thing to do is to find a special place to put it, following some important considerations.

The Computer Table

The computer should be put on a table that places the keyboard at a good height for your students. For instance, a typewriter table, which stands 26 inches off the ground, is a good height for most fifth graders to high schoolers.

The monitor should be placed at eye level, either right on top of the computer or to the side on building blocks. Many commercially made computer tables have a shelf built above the level where the computer sits that sets the monitor 6 or 10 inches above the keyboard. This is not acceptable for students until they have grown to their adult height. Remove this shelf and place the monitor on top of the computer. This will be much more comfortable.

Also, if you need a movable station, you will probably want wheels on your computer table. Keep in mind that these wheels add extra height to the table.

For youngsters in the lower grades, a table should be adjusted to hold the keyboard 2 inches lower than the average desk used at each particular grade. For example, in a second grade room, the average desk height is 26 inches, so a good height for the computer keyboard would be 24 inches. Cut 2 inches off the legs of a table. Trying to use a smaller desk that has a shelf for storing books will not work because students will not be able to get their legs under the desk top.

If the computer is going to be used by students in different grades, it will be tricky to get furniture that will be suitable for all of them. Since students need to sit so that the screen is at eye level, look into pneumatic chairs that adjust. If there is a footstool or a shoe box on the floor in front of the chair for the smaller children to rest their feet on, they should be comfortable.

The table should be wide enough to accommodate a disk drive and printer and any other peripherals that are needed. There should also be enough desk-top space for a work area where students can put their papers or worksheets for an assignment.

Lighting and Electricity

An important consideration is lighting. Study the lighting to see that there is no glare on the monitor screen from overhead lights or windows. Make sure that the computer is not in a dark corner.

Make sure that there are electric outlets for the computer, its monitor, and the printer, and enough outlets if you have more than one machine. The wires should be located so that no one will trip over them.

Creating a Private Place

You might want to create a cubicle for the computer to give the working student some privacy and to keep other students in the room from being distracted by the computer.

An informal cubicle can be made with a partition made from a washing machine or refrigerator carton that has been opened down the side and covered with contact paper. Place the computer table against the wall and place the partition behind the student and around the table. The student working at the computer will not only be using business applications but will also feel like a member of the business world in this special office.

Using Part of the Classroom Space

If there are several computers in the classroom, the same consideration must be given to having appropriate furniture and lighting. It may be more difficult, however, to provide privacy.

Usually in this situation the teacher lines up tables against the back wall so that the students using the computers have their backs to the rest of the class. Students usually enjoy working next to each other on the computer. Because of their natural curiosity, they may become interested in each other's activities. Sometimes they learn from each other. Still, you should make sure that they are not so close that they do not do their own work or that they don't have enough room to spread out their materials.

WHEN THERE IS A LAB

Since, in a lab situation, everyone is working on a computer, the teacher is free to arrange the room in any fashion. A common arrangement is to set the tables up in a U shape with the students facing out. The students have their backs to the teacher, but the teacher can see what is happening on each monitor.

STORING MANUALS

Always keep the manuals that come with your computer and software programs on the computer table or on a shelf next to the computer. Students should be encouraged to use the manuals for reference. A handy way to store your manuals is between bookends. Less space is used, and when there is a specific place for things to be put, students are naturally neater.

Label a section for manuals, one for computer magazines, and another for books on computers or any other support materials you may have. The result will be a small library of the most important references the students can have in the computer area.

In a situation where there are three or four computers, you may want to set up a central location for your computer library. Some tables or computer desks have an area for materials under the table top. You may want to keep your materials there.

BULLETIN BOARDS AND DISPLAYS

It is important to have a pleasing environment. Ask the students to help in planning bulletin boards and displays that are not only neat and attractive but also supportive to the projects that are your main objective.

As an example, if a student is working on a project that requires that she input her birthdate, there should be a display close by that shows the exact format that she should follow (05/15/74 or May 15, 1974). Charts with detailed directions for the assignment and the editing commands that will be used are most important and should be posted near the student.

Samples of students' work should be posted whenever possible.

SCHEDULING

Scheduling is perhaps the most important aspect of a successful classroom computer program because you want to make maximum use of the hardware. One approach is to assign time slots for each student. You can post these times on a chart, and students will know they are to use the computer during their assigned time. This type of scheduling works well when you have students who need to leave the room for music lessons or special instruction because you can put these students in slots that do not interfere with their special activities.

It's difficult, though, to know exactly how long to make the time slots, which may be a drawback to this type of scheduling. It may be frustrating for students to begin a project they are excited about and then be asked to wait several days before they can work on their project again. One possibility is to provide free computer time during the lunch hour or before and after school.

Another way of scheduling is to have a folder for each student. When the day begins, the student whose folder is on the top of the pile goes to the computer first. If there is a specific assignment, the teacher judges what should be done at this time and the student works until it is completed. When finished, that student tells the student whose folder is next that he or she can go to the computer. A student aide is helpful in this plan because the aide can monitor the time students are taking and offer assistance if it is needed.

After each session, students place in their folders all of the printed work that they have accomplished and record other work on a log sheet stapled to the inside of the folders. These folders are placed in another pile, and when it is convenient, the teacher can review the work, comment, return the printed material to the students, and add the folders to the bottom of the original pile. This system is more flexible than assigned time slots, and it encourages the students to keep all of their work together.

Sign-up sheets are effective if there are times, other than class time, when students who want more "on-time" can use the computers. Teachers who arrive early in the morning and stay late after school make computer "whiz kids" very happy. Lunch hours are also good sign-up times. Using a form, the teacher fills in the times that he or she will be available, and then students, on a first-come-first-served basis, sign up for the times that are convenient for them.

If students want to team up, they can each sign up for a block of time and then work together for both blocks. For example, two children in the primary grades might each sign up for 30 minutes and work together for an hour.

STUDENT COMPUTER AIDES

Whatever way you choose to schedule, be sure that it is a plan that demands the least of your teaching time once the assignments have been carefully explained. Using student computer aides is an effective way to achieve this.

Select a student or group of students to serve as computer aides. These may be children who have previous computer experience or seem to learn computer skills rapidly.

Take the time to give them specialized training. Run through each assignment with them and be sure that they have successfully completed it before the other students seek their help. Using students as aides can be significantly helpful to teachers. The teacher's role should be to initiate and to motivate, and the aide's role should be to help facilitate the activity.

ABOUT DISKETTES

Disk Storage and Usage

Floppy disks are fragile and can be destroyed if they are not properly cared for. Ground rules for proper use of the computer and care of diskettes should be discussed before the students work with them. Floppy disks should always be put into their half envelopes and then stored in a dust-free container.

If you are working on only a few computer activities for the year, you might want to have several students share the same diskette. But if you are giving them many opportunities throughout the year, you should have a disk for each student. If cost is a problem, refer to the several fund-raising activities discussed in this book for suggestions and then get the class rolling on a fund-raising project.

Have the students label their diskettes using the labels that come with the boxes of blank disks. They should write their names on a label *before* affixing it. If it becomes necessary to write on the label when it is already on the diskette, use a felt-tipped pen. Ball-point pens make indentations and can destroy the diskette.

If you are working with very young children, you may want to boot the system yourself each morning and assign a "helper" to change disks as necessary during the day. Older students should be permitted to change the data disks themselves because this is a part of the learning process.

Maintaining Sanity with Disks

Unless you take precautions, you will soon be drowning in a sea of disks. They seem to multiply themselves like amoebas. Plan for storage in advance. All disks should be stored in dust-proof boxes; order some, perhaps two, 50-disk containers.

You will have two kinds of disks: program disks and data disks.

A *program disk* is the one that has instructions to the computer on it. (Bank Street Writer, PFS File and PFS Report, and FlashCalc are examples of programs.) After they have been used to give the computer instructions, they can be put back in their container. You should *never* write or save on a program disk.

If there is no write-protect tab covering the cutout on the side of the disk, put one on immediately. (Write-protect tabs are the silver, gold, or black sticky tabs that come in all boxes of blank disks.) You should never present a student with a program disk that is not write-protected.

A *data disk* is one on which you save your own information--your own compositions, lists, or budget. These begin as blank diskettes, which you buy usually in boxes of ten. Each one has to be *initialized,* or formatted, through BASIC or through the program itself before it can be used. There is an initializing operation in Bank Street Writer, PFS File, and FlashCalc. Many Bank Street Writer and FlashCalc projects can be kept on the same data disk. However, on the Apple, each PFS file requires its own data disk.

DISKETTES AND *BASIC*

The following instructions are for the Apple. If you are using an IBM PC or a PCjr, please refer to Appendix A.

Initializing a Data Disk Through BASIC

If you do not know how to initialize a data disk through BASIC, the following will be helpful to you. Just follow these steps:

1. Place the System Master disk that came with your computer into the disk drive and turn the computer on.
2. Wait for the drive to stop whirring.
3. Remove the disk from the drive and place a blank disk, right out of the box, into the drive.

4. At the prompt (]) type the following little program. Be sure to press the RETURN key at the end of each line.

```
NEW
 5 REM HELLO
10 PRINT "DISK FOR (use your name)'S CLASS"
20 PRINT "CREATED ON (use today's date)"
30 PRINT "DISK# (give it a number or unique  name)"
40 END
```

5. Now type the following and press RETURN.

```
INIT HELLO
```

The computer will now initialize the blank disk. It will divide the disk's surface into tracks and those tracks into sectors. It will also create a *catalog*, or directory, for itself so that it will be able to find rapidly the information you save on the disk.

Be sure that all disks are well marked. Write on the label before putting it onto the disk. If you ever have to write on a disk, always use a felt-tipped pen. Ballpoint pens and pencils can destroy disks.

Copying a Disk Using COPYA

Many program disks cannot be copied; they have been "protected" during the manufacturing process. But all data disks can and should be copied because disks are easily damaged. You cannot read data off damaged disks. A whole class's work can be lost because of a speck of dust.

We recommend that you use the COPYA program on the System Master disk that came with your computer. Follow these steps:

• Insert your System Master in Drive 1 and close the door. (If you have only one drive, put the System Master into it.)
• Turn on the monitor and then the computer. The disk will boot.
• At the prompt (]), type **COPYA** and press RETURN. (The computer will read the COPYA program off the System Master disk and into memory.)
• Read the following, and then proceed with the instructions depending on the number of disk drives that you have.

You will now be asked to designate the slot and drive for the *source diskette* (the one you wish to copy) and the *target diskette* (the blank disk to be copied onto). These are defaulted at Slot 6, Drive 1 for the source diskette, and Slot 6, Drive 2 for the target diskette.

The word *default* means that the person who wrote the program preselected the most common answer to a question or choice that you, the user, will be presented with. This is to make your work easier. However, a default can be changed. The change that you might make now is if you have only one disk drive: You will need to change the target drive from Drive 2 to Drive 1. (With two disk drives, the defaulted target drive is correct, so no change needs to be made. And with either one or two disk drives, your drives are probably plugged into Slot 6, so that default will also remain unchanged.)

Depending on how many disk drives you have, now continue with the instructions below.

Copying with two disk drives:
*   Accept all the defaults by hitting RETURN four times.
*   Remove the System Master from Drive 1 and put it away. Place the disk you wish to copy in Drive 1. Place the blank disk in Drive 2.
*   Press RETURN, as instructed, to begin the copying procedure.
*   When the computer is finished, it will ask if you wish to make additional copies. Type **Y** or **N**, depending on whether your choice is Yes or No to making additional copies.

Copying with one disk drive:
*   Hit RETURN three times, type **1**, and press RETURN again. This will tell the computer that both your source and target disks will be in Drive 1--that you have only one drive.
*   Now, remove the System Master from the drive and put it away. Place the disk you wish to copy in the drive. Keep the blank disk close at hand.
*   Press RETURN to begin the copying procedure. The computer will ask you to switch disks every few moments as it copies the programs from the disk.
*   When the computer is finished, it will ask if you wish to make additional copies. Type **Y** or **N**, depending upon whether your choice to make another copy is Yes or No.

OBJECTIVES FOR SUCCESS

Once the hardware is in place and your software is in order, it is time to select the objectives for your specific class and to find activities that relate to these objectives. The goal of this book is to provide you with these tools.

It is important to have a feel for the level of computer competence of each of your students. Some may have never touched a computer, particularly in the lower grades, and others may know more than you do. But few, at least in the beginning, will be familiar with the types of projects that you will be introducing from this book.

Your first objective will be to ensure that all of your students know how to turn the computer on and off and how to load and run software packages. You want them to be comfortable working with the computer. Peer tutors, in addition to student computer aides, can be very helpful. You might select peer tutors from your aides, from children in the class who are very familiar with computers, or from children in slightly higher grades. Fourth graders who already know Bank Street Writer, for instance, can teach it to second graders.

Each time you present an activity, make sure that you have given careful instructions and have called attention to any support materials that are available in the room for reference. You want the learner to experience success. Be sure that the directions you give are specific and complete and place a written copy of your directions near the computer.

As you monitor the students' computer activities, you may find that some are not completing the assignment even after several opportunities at the computer. You may have to bring this group together for further assistance.

Chapter 2
Wordprocessing

Processing words is something we do all day long as we seek to understand one another, to communicate ideas, and to express our thoughts and feelings--in the best words and most effective style we can find. Finding the right words and sorting through the many choices of diction, grammar, and syntax available to us is the sort of wordprocessing we all do without calling it by that name.

WHY A COMPUTER?

A wordprocessor is a tool for improving our competency in communicating. It is simply a programmed set of instructions that allows a writer to type in text with a keyboard; make insertions and deletions, move about, and otherwise revise this text; save it onto a disk for future revision or reference; and print out drafts or final copies.

Such a program allows us to increase our fluency in expressing thoughts and feelings because it puts our text on screen in easily readable and scannable form, permits all sorts of corrections without yielding copy sloppy with erasures and overwriting, only does what we instruct it to do--and is a patient observer of the composing process. We are freed of the drudgery of recopying a draft, freed of the worry about our penmanship, and freed to experiment with our writing until we get it right.

THE PROJECTS

Project 1 teaches, step by step, how to use Bank Street Writer, a very effective wordprocessing program for children. This project actually has three parts.

The additional seven projects promise adventure and imaginative products. For these projects, Bank Street Writer or any other wordprocessor will do.

The "Creature from Outer Space," Project 2, stretches the imagination, as does "From a Pet's Point of View," which is Project 3. "How Did It Happen?" Project 4, requires the writer to answer typical reporter's questions from a personal point of view. "Tying a Shoelace," Project 5, encourages students to give step-by-step instructions for a simple task they can write and they can test. The "Soap Opera," Project 6, is a community project involving the entire class. Kids are all expert about many things: In Project 7, the class has a chance to prove what experts they are. And, Project 8 provides an opportunity to develop an understanding of the differences between advertising, public relations, and news reporting.

All of the ideas introduced in the projects are exciting writing ideas for student compositions. They are, however, most suited to using a wordprocessor because they demonstrate the value of being able to make changes easily: developing the kernel of the idea, expanding it into an outline, developing thoughts from the outline, and deleting and expanding as the total composition takes form. All the work with little pain. The result: an attractive and well-thought-out writing product.

Getting Started
with Bank Street Writer

Requires: **Bank Street Writer**

Bank Street Writer is a wordprocessing program that allows you to type your written work onto the screen, change this text, save it onto a floppy disk, and then print out the results. Both Scholastic and Broderbund market Bank Street Writer, and for our purposes the two versions work the same.

To *boot* Bank Street Writer, that is to copy the program from the floppy disk into the memory of the microcomputer, first insert the Bank Street Writer program disk into the disk drive (Drive 1 if you have more than one drive attached to your computer). Do this carefully, holding the program disk by its label and putting it in the drive label side up, oval first. Close the door of the drive.

Next, turn on the monitor and then the microcomputer. The disk drive's red IN USE light will go on and a whirring sound will be audible as the disk revolves within. During this time, do not open the door of the drive to remove the disk, for this will damage the disk. When all of the program is copied into the memory of the computer, the light will go off and the sound will no longer be audible. Since the entire Bank Street Writer program is now within the memory of the computer, the program disk need not remain in the disk drive. Remove the program disk from the drive and put it away for safekeeping.

ENTERING TEXT

On the screen, you first see the name of the program and its copyright information. Follow the prompts on the screen to get to the first composing screen, which is labeled ENTER TEXT. When this screen is before you, text may be entered, up to 39 letters, numbers, or symbols across the screen. The *cursor*, the flashing rectangle that moves across the screen as characters are entered, shows where on the screen the next typed character will go.

In the ENTER TEXT mode, you may delete the last character or characters typed by hitting the LEFT ARROW key once for each character. It does not let you go back to an earlier part of your work to make corrections without deleting the text in between. So the ENTER TEXT mode is really a place to type in your ideas without great concern for typing accuracy or absolute correctness. Fixing up the text comes later.

To practice using Bank Street Writer, you need to type in some text. You may use the story below about Ralph the Hamster. Keep the following directions in mind as you type.

•   When you get to the end of a line on the screen, keep typing. Bank Street
    Writer will *wrap around* a word that does not fit on the line, that is, move it

around to the beginning of the next line.
- If you wish to go on to a new line before you reach the right-hand edge of the screen, hit the RETURN key.
- If you wish to skip a line, also hit the RETURN key.
- If you make a typing error, use the LEFT ARROW key to delete it, but not if the error is several lines above.
- If you notice an error several lines above, don't use the LEFT ARROW key because you'll delete all your typing between where you are and where the error is. Just leave the mistakes for now: No harm's done.

Now type Ralph's story exactly as it appears below.

The Hang Gliding Hamster

Once there was a hamster called Ralph.
Ralph was an unusual hamster. When he
was two, his parents, who were also
unusual, taught him how to hang glide.

Ralph worked a long time on his first
hang glider. It was made of an envelope
and paper clips. It was plain white,
which Ralph did not like. After he
learned how to make better hang
gliders, he added color.

Ralph was clever. He learned how to
open his cage by himself. He would
stand on its top and whoosh--glide
across the room. Ralph liked how it
felt to hang in the air, to see
everything below him.

After using 18 lines of space on the screen, you will see the text scroll upward to make room for additional text. All of the words you have typed are still in the microcomputer's memory, even if you cannot see them all.

Ralph was quite content to be the
world's only hamster hang glider.
He even went to the Olympics. The
opposing teams had no hamsters like
himself, so Ralph won the gold, silver,
and bronze medals. He took them
home and lived glidingly ever after.

MAKING CHANGES IN THE TEXT

Now that you have typed in the story, you need to look it over. Perhaps you would like to change the story--add some interesting material, remove some of the words, correct typing errors. In order to change text in Ralph's story or in any other piece of writing you do with Bank Street Writer, you must move from the ENTER TEXT mode into the EDIT mode. Hit the ESC (Escape) key at the upper left-hand corner of the keyboard.

In EDIT mode, you will see a *menu*, or list, of seven commands: ERASE, UNERASE, MOVE, MOVEBACK, FIND, REPLACE, and TRANSFER MENU. These are for operations that you will do as you proceed through the process of learning how to use Bank Street Writer. You will get to them shortly. First, however, you will make some simple corrections.

Using Cursor Movement Keys

Now that you are in EDIT mode, you may move your cursor to where there are errors in Ralph's story. There is a total of eight ways you may move, and in some cases, how you carry out each move depends on whether you are using an Apple II+, or an Apple//e or //c keyboard. Try the method for your computer as described:

On the Apple II+, to move:
left a character at a time, use the J key
right a character at a time, use the K key
down a line at a time, use the M key
up a line at a time, use the I key

To speed up the process, hold down the letter key and also press the RPT (Repeat) key. This will move the cursor more quickly.

On the Apple//e and Apple//c, to move:
left a character at a time, press the LEFT ARROW key
right a character at a time, use the RIGHT ARROW key
down a line at a time, press the DOWN ARROW key
up a line at a time, press the UP ARROW key

To have the key repeat, hold it down. This will give you speedy movement.

On all keyboards, to move:
to the beginning of the text, hit the B key (B for beginning)
to the end of the text, hit the E key (E for end)
down 12 lines on the screen, hit the D key (D for down)
up 12 lines on the screen, hit the U key (U for up)

Deleting Unwanted Text

You may wish to delete characters or words from the text.

- In EDIT mode, move your cursor under the first character you wish to delete, then hit ESC to enter WRITE OR CORRECT mode. (What is WRITE OR CORRECT mode? It is the new name given to ENTER mode after you have left it for EDIT mode. Bank Street Writer assumes that you are done composing in ENTER mode after you hit ESC, and that you will return to your work to make revisions.)
- Use the RIGHT ARROW key to delete this character and any others following it that you wish to delete.
- To delete a character in another place in the text, hit ESC again to enter EDIT mode, use your cursor movement keys to move the cursor under the character you wish to delete, hit ESC, then delete with the RIGHT ARROW key.

You may try this with Ralph's story. In EDIT mode, move your cursor to the third line of the second paragraph. Put the cursor under the letter **p** in the word **plain**. Hit ESC to return to WRITE OR CORRECT mode. Delete all five letters in the word by hitting the right arrow key five times.

Now hit ESC again. Move to the third line of the final paragraph with the D key and either the M key or the DOWN ARROW key. Move the cursor with the RIGHT ARROW key or the K key to the first letter in the word **even**. Hit ESC to get out of EDIT MODE and into WRITE OR CORRECT mode. Use the RIGHT ARROW key to delete all four letters of this word.

Note for Apple//e and Apple//c users: You have probably realized that the LEFT and RIGHT ARROW keys have two functions: they delete text in ENTER or WRITE OR CORRECT modes, and they move the cursor left or right in EDIT mode.

Work at deleting all the typing errors you may have made when typing in Ralph's story so that when you are done you have gained confidence in cursor movement and deletion.

Inserting New Text

You have now deleted typing errors, but what if you wish to insert a letter or word that you left out? Once again, you need to move between EDIT and WRITE OR CORRECT modes using the ESC key and move about the screen with your cursor movement keys.

Let's give Ralph a color. Be sure you are in EDIT mode (the top left-hand corner of the screen will say so). Now, move your cursor to the **h** in the word **hamster** in the first line of the story. What color hamster is Ralph? Hit ESC and insert your color word. Notice that all the rest of the text moves over to allow space for this inserted word.

Hit ESC to return to EDIT mode and move to the comma after the word **two** in the third line of this same paragraph. Hit ESC again and type in the words **years old**.

Hit ESC again. Move to another spot in the text where you omitted to type a letter or word and type in your correction. Work through your text until Ralph's story contains all the characters and words it should.

Leave the computer on and take a short break before continuing.

New Operations
with Bank Street Writer

Requires: **Bank Street Writer**

CENTERING TEXT

Let's go back to Ralph's story. "The Hang Gliding Hamster" is a good title for this story, but wouldn't it look better centered on the page? You can center this title with ease.

- Be sure you are in EDIT mode.
- Move your cursor to under the **T** in **The**.
- Hit ESC to return to WRITE OR CORRECT mode.
- Now, while you hold down the CTRL key, hit the C (for center) key. Release both keys.

A banner with the word **Center** will appear and **The Hang Gliding Hamster** will appear right in the middle of the line. Of course, when you print your story, the banner will not show up.

USING THE EDIT MODE MENU

The EDIT mode has seven choices in its *menu*, or list of commands. You will use ERASE, UNERASE, MOVE, MOVEBACK, FIND, and REPLACE to make major changes in your text and TRANSFER MENU when it is time to save and print your work.

To select one of the seven choices from the EDIT mode menu, you must move the highlighter to that choice, then hit RETURN to lock in that choice. There are three keys that move the highlighter:

On the Apple II+, to move:
one choice to the right, use the RIGHT ARROW key
one choice to the left, use the LEFT ARROW key
from row to row, use the SPACE bar

On the Apple//e or //c, to move:
one choice to the right, use the SOLID APPLE key
one choice to the left, use the HOLLOW APPLE key
from row to row, use the SPACE bar

Remember to hit the RETURN key to lock in your choice. Hit ESC to cancel a mistaken choice.

Using ERASE and UNERASE

There are times when you want to erase more than a character or a word at a time. To speed up the process, use ERASE. You may erase up to 15 lines of text at one time. Larger pieces of text can be erased in 15-line segments.

Let's practice using ERASE and UNERASE with Ralph's story. Suppose you decide to erase the words **who were also unusual** from the last two lines of the first paragraph of the story.

- First, be sure you are in EDIT mode.
- Highlight ERASE and hit RETURN.
- Move the cursor to the **w** in the word **who** and hit RETURN.
- Then using the RIGHT ARROW key or the K key move the cursor to mark, or highlight, the four words you wish to erase.
- Hit RETURN again. Then type **Y**, for yes, you want to erase the four words. (Please note that you are guided throughout this operation with cues in the form of questions along the top of the screen.)

You might decide that you wanted those four words in the story after all. You can put them back immediately after erasing by using UNERASE.

Before hitting any other key, move the highlighter to UNERASE. Hit the RETURN key to lock in this choice. Answer **Y** to UNERASE the words and--Voila!--they are back.

Using MOVE and MOVEBACK

These two choices work very much the same as ERASE and UNERASE, only now you can move up to 15 lines of text from one place in your text to another. If you change your mind and have not hit any other key after using MOVE, then you may MOVEBACK the text. You may move large chunks of text in 15-line segments until the entire chunk is moved.

Let's practice MOVE and MOVEBACK with Ralph's story. The second and third paragraphs of his story can be reversed and still tell an orderly story. So, let's move the second paragraph so that it becomes the third paragraph.

- Be sure you are in EDIT mode.
- Highlight MOVE and press RETURN.
- Move the cursor to the first letter of the second paragraph, the **R** in **Ralph**, and hit RETURN.
- Highlight the entire paragraph by moving the cursor down and right. When you have highlighted the entire paragraph, hit RETURN.
- Now move your cursor to the space between paragraphs three and four and hit RETURN to indicate that this is where you wish to MOVE the paragraph to.
- You are asked if you are sure. Press **Y** for yes.

The paragraph is moved!

But, if you decide to MOVEBACK the paragraph because you don't like the change, before hitting any other key, highlight MOVEBACK and press RETURN. Answer **Y** that you wish to MOVEBACK the text, and it is done.

Using FIND and REPLACE

These two choices from the EDIT menu allow you to FIND all the appearances of a word or series of words up to 29 characters long, and REPLACE them with some other word or words.

Bank Street Writer will find what you direct it to, in exactly the form you tell it. Thus, if you ask it to find the word **the**, it will find all of the occurrences of **the** in your text, but it will also find all of the words that have the string of characters **the** in them, such as **them, other,** and **bathe.** To avoid this kind of confusion, put a space before and after the word you wish to find. Also, Bank Street Writer distinguishes between upper and lower case, so when you are looking for **the**, you will not find **The.**

Let's use FIND in Ralph's story.

- First, be sure that your cursor is at the beginning of the story.
- Type **B** (for beginning) in EDIT mode.
- Move the highlighter to FIND and hit RETURN.
- Answer the prompt with the word you want to find in the story, perhaps the word **hamster**, and press RETURN. (Remember to place spaces around the word.)
- Type **Y** to search for all appearances of the chosen word.

The computer will FIND and highlight each occurrence.

Now, let's change Ralph's name. You can change one word or a group of words of up to 29 characters using REPLACE.

- Be sure you are in EDIT mode and make sure that your cursor is at the beginning of the story.
- Highlight REPLACE and press RETURN.
- The computer will ask you what word to FIND. Type **Ralph** and press RETURN.
- To the question of what you want to REPLACE it with, fill in your answer-- **Michael, Maya, Princess?**--and press RETURN.

Your hamster has a new name!

Transfer Menu
with Bank Street Writer

Requires: **Bank Street Writer**
Printer

So far, all we have done is manipulate our words on the screen. But the process becomes really valuable when we can transfer our work to paper.

The final choice in EDIT mode is TRANSFER MENU. Highlight this selection, and press RETURN. You are now in the TRANSFER MENU. A new screen appears which contains nine choices: RETRIEVE, SAVE, INIT, DELETE, RENAME, PRINT-DRAFT, PRINT-FINAL, QUIT, and CLEAR.

INITIALIZING DATA DISKS

Let's begin with INIT, which means to initialize. All data disks must be initialized before they can be used. They must be told how information is going to be organized on that disk. (With IBM systems, the word *format* is used for the same operation.) There is a program within Bank Street Writer that allows us to do that. If you do not have an already initialized diskette in Drive 1, place a blank disk in the drive. Highlight INIT. *(Make sure your Bank Street Writer program disk is not in the drive. You could destroy it with this operation.)* Now, press RETURN.

The light on the drive will go on. Whatever is on the disk is being completely overwritten, and the disk is being prepared to accept your Bank Street Writer compositions. Do not open the drive door until the light goes off and the whirring sound has stopped.

You now have an initialized diskette. Make a label for it and then put the label on the disk. Never write directly onto the disk. Place the disk back into Drive 1.

MANIPULATING FILES

Saving Files

Now, you may save Ralph's story onto the disk. First, highlight SAVE and press RETURN. You will be asked a series of questions:

> **SAVE ENTIRE FILE? (Y/N):** You probably want to save all of it.
> Answer **Y**.
> **DO YOU WANT A CATALOG? (Y/N):** A catalog is a list of all the
> other files on the disk. Since there are none, this being the first, type **N**.

18

TYPE NAME OF FILE TO SAVE: Now, give the file a name. A name can be up to eight (8) characters long with no punctuation or spaces. "Ralph" is a good name. Type **Ralph** and press RETURN. (If you use a name that already resides on the disk, the computer will write over the old copy--so keep using different names.)

RALPH will be saved to the disk. You may repeat the SAVE process onto another initialized disk. This will provide you with a backup copy in case anything happens to the first disk.

Retrieving Files

RETRIEVE works almost the same way as SAVE. It allows you to load a file from a data disk into the memory of the computer. Let's say that tomorrow you want to work on Ralph again. You would do the following:

- Start with the Bank Street Writer disk.
- Proceed to TRANSFER MENU and select it.
- Highlight RETRIEVE.
- Type in the name of the file you wish to see and press RETURN. (You might ask for a catalog to make sure that you have the right spelling.)

Now, if you type **Ralph** and press RETURN, Ralph's story will appear on the screen.

Renaming Files

When you want to RENAME a file, you tell the computer the old name that resides on the disk and then the new name. The computer will change the name of the file on the disk.

PRINTING

Using PRINT-DRAFT

PRINT-DRAFT prints the file exactly as it appears on the screen, that is, 39 characters per line. To use PRINT-DRAFT, you must answer some of the same questions listed in PRINT-FINAL. PRINT-DRAFT helps you to find errors before you do a final copy, and because it prints as the copy appears on the screen, it helps you to find the error on the screen.

Using PRINT-FINAL

PRINT-FINAL allows you to determine how your text will print out--what space there is to be between lines, how many characters across a line. Bank Street

Writer asks you a series of questions. There are defaults for each question, which are the most common answers. The first time you print Ralph's story, accept the defaults. Then go in and make changes as you see fit.

Here are the questions that will appear on your screen:

How many characters per line?   65
Spacing between lines?   1 prints single spaced, 2 prints double spaced
Is this a continuation of the previous file?   N
Pages to be numbered?   Y
Start at page #?   1
Pause between pages? N (Y if single sheet paper)
Eject Last Page? Y
Type in Page Heading: (Use this if you want a heading.)
Print Entire File? Y
Do you want to see where each page of text will end? N (If you
   want to, press **Y**, and use the I and M or UP/DOWN ARROW keys to
   adjust a page break.)

When you have answered all the questions, prepare to print. If in the process of printing, you want to stop, press ESC.

EXITING

Clearing the Memory

CLEAR erases the memory of the computer, allowing you to start a new file. Use CLEAR only after you have saved the file in memory onto a disk.

Quitting

Use QUIT to exit from Bank Street Writer and to return to BASIC.

You are ready to create your own files on Bank Street Writer. If you are ever confused, check the manual that came with the program. Happy writing!

The Creature from Outer Space

Requires: **Bank Street Writer** or another wordprocessing program
         Printer

Movies and television show us alien beings. But have you ever tried to draw with words how you imagine such visitors might look? Perhaps you have a picture already in your mind, but if you don't--or if you want to fix up your picture--ask yourself these questions.

> How is my alien shaped? Is it shaped like a person? Like an insect or a bird? Like some form that we don't see on earth?
> How big is my alien? Or how small? And, what colors? What is its texture-- smooth or rough, soft or hard?
> How does my alien communicate? Does it have its own language of sounds or movements? What does it want me to know?

Asking yourself questions like these is a good start for writing a description of your alien--or any other creature, thing, person, object--because it gets you thinking and imagining, and then good ideas flow.

Taking Notes

Start up your Bank Street Writer disk and use the screen as a notebook to jot down the answers you have to these many questions. Save these ideas to a file on an initialized, or formatted, disk and call this file ALIEN1. Then take a break from thinking about your alien.

Come back to writing about your alien some hours later or the next day and retrieve your file ALIEN1. Read over your ideas to see how good they feel to you. Pick out the two or three ideas that you like the best and remember these. Clear your screen. Your file ALIEN1 is still on your formatted disk if you wish to read over your ideas again.

Getting the Ideas Down

Now begin writing out each of your ideas, one at a time. Write a whole lot on one idea if you like, because this means your imagination is fired by this idea. Then write about the next idea, and the next. You may discover as you write that you have lots of new ideas, ideas that you hadn't thought of before--and this is a wonderful situation to be in.

But what if you can't seem to think of anything at all to write about? Hmmm. Really, this seldom happens. More likely, you will write something, but not as much as you would like. If what you have written is interesting to you, even if it is brief, then it is good. But if you still wish to write more, try this: Imagine you are the only person who has seen the alien and you have to describe it to your best friend. What would you need to write to make your friend see the alien as well as you do?

Making It Better

Now that you have written a good deal about the alien, save your writing to the formatted disk under the file name ALIEN2. You probably like some parts of your writing better than others. Use Bank Street Writer's ERASE command to erase the parts you are no longer interested in (you have a copy in ALIEN2 just in case you change your mind!), and look carefully at what remains. Ask yourself if there are ways you can improve your description.

> Have you described your alien so that you've either started with the whole of him or her and worked down to details or begun with an important detail and worked your way up to the whole of him or her?
> Are there more descriptive words you can add to make the picture of your alien clearer?
> Have you finished the thought in each of your sentences and written more than one sentence for each paragraph?
> Finally, how are your spelling and punctuation?

When you are happy with your word drawing of the alien, save it to your formatted disk as a file called ALIEN3. Then use Bank Street Writer's PRINT-FINAL command to print out your description of the alien.

From a Pet's Point of View

Requires: **Bank Street Writer** or another wordprocessing program
Printer

Probably all of us have a pet (or several pets!) or are friends with someone else who does. We observe our pets carefully and can tell delightful stories about their idiosyncracies. But have you ever wondered how our pets look at us as we are busily caring for them, delighting in playing with them? Do you suppose that pets find our ways of behaving quite peculiar--or charming, or silly? Were a pet to tell you a story about its master, how do you suppose it would go?

To help you get started, here are some questions you might ask yourself:

Which pet should I write about? My own? Someone else's? An imaginary pet (for those of you who have always wanted a bronze dragon)?
What kind of person, I mean pet, is this pet? What is its personality like? Does it like lasagna more than anything, or chasing a ball?
What are the most important things in the life of this pet?
How does this pet see its master? In a loving way? In a bored way? In a funny way?

These questions and others you think of yourself will help you imagine how it feels to be this pet and how things look from its point of view. Try thinking as if you yourself were this pet.

Taking Notes

Now start up your Bank Street Writer disk and use the screen as a notebook to jot down the answers you have to these questions and others you ask yourself. Save these nifty ideas to a formatted disk in a file called PET1. Go and treat yourself to a snack.

Later, retrieve your file PET1 and read over your ideas. Some will still seem nifty, others less so. Pick out a few ideas you especially like and clear your screen. PET1 is still saved on your formatted disk, and you can go back to it any time you wish.

Starting to Write

Now begin writing on each of your ideas, one at a time. If one idea brings up new ideas, go with them, for sometimes the best ideas don't come at the start of writing, but after thinking and writing awhile.

What if you're having trouble getting started? Maybe you've selected the wrong pet. Think for a moment of some pet you would really like to have and why you'd really like to have it. Then imagine how such a pet would feel to have such a caring owner--and you're on your way again.

Telling a Story

Now that you've written a good deal from the pet's point of view, maybe you've decided it would be fun to tell a story about something that happened to this pet--and tell the story of how the pet felt when it happened.

Or perhaps you've decided to have this pet talk in its own voice (not barking or meowing, I don't mean that) if the pet could speak English. These are two enjoyable ways of writing about your chosen pet.

Go back through what you've written so that all your ideas become part of how you are telling this pet's story--and do away with, ERASE, all those ideas that, even though they are fine, just don't fit this particular story.

Making it Better

Ask yourself if there are ways you can improve on your story:

Should you describe where it takes place in more detail, or add a longer description of your pet's owner, or let your pet go on and on about how terrific he thinks he is?

Look through your sentences to make sure each feels finished, that it completes a thought.

Then check for correct spelling and punctuation.

When you are through, save your writing to the formatted disk in a file called PET3. Then use a PRINT-FINAL to make a paper copy of your story to share with your class.

How Did It Happen?

Requires: **Bank Street Writer** or another wordprocessing program
           Printer

The glass fish tank lies shattered on the floor. Water runs to all corners of the room. Lying quite still is Harold, a newly purchased goldfish. There are four witnesses to the scene:

    Fred Jones, a professional basketball player
    Jane Smith, a veterinarian
    Bobby Collins, an eleven-year-old boy
    Cindy Daniels, a twelve-year-old girl

    Your job is to tell what happened from the point of view of one of these four people, that is, through the eyes of one of them.

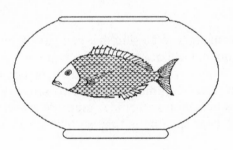

Taking Notes

    To begin, select the person whose story you wish to tell. Now start your Bank Street Writer program, and using the computer screen as a notebook, record all of your ideas about this person and his or her version of the story. If you discover that you wish you had chosen to write about another person, simply clear your screen and begin again.
    To help you get going, here are some ideas:

    Imagine the kind of person Fred, Jane, Bobby, or Cindy is.
    Imagine what your person has to do with Harold, the goldfish.
    Imagine when your person last saw Harold.
    Imagine where your person was when Harold hit the ground.
    Imagine how your person would explain Harold's end.

When you are finished taking notes, save your file as FRED1, JANE1, BOBBY1, or CINDY1. Then take a break and let your mind wander to other subjects. You may discover when you return to work that you have come back with some interesting new ideas.

What Really Happened to Harold?

Now it is time to tell your person's version of Harold's demise. You may even try telling the story in the first person, that is, as if your person were speaking in his or her own voice. When you are through, take a well-earned break. But before doing so, save your work as FRED2, JANE2, BOBBY2, or CINDY2.

Fixing up your story is the last stage of your writing task, for you need to make the story as clear to others as it is to you, and this requires that you make clear all the steps in the story that led to Harold's demise. Be sure that you can answer the journalist's questions:

> What happened?
> Where did it happen?
> When did it happen?
> How did it happen?
> Why did it happen?

Making It Better

Now look through your story to be sure that you have selected the best words to explain your ideas. You may choose to change a word or two so that your word choices are more varied. You may decide to expand a sentence with more words to make its ideas more complete. You may connect two sentences to combine their ideas. Check over your punctuation so that idea units are properly separated, as are items in lists. Make sure your spelling is fine, so that others will be able to read your words with ease.

Now save your work as FRED3, JANE3, BOBBY 3, or CINDY3, and make a final print. You've done a good job!

Tying Shoelaces

Requires: **Bank Street Writer** or another wordprocessing program
        Printer

Writing down the process by which you do something is not as easy as you would
think because we do a lot of things without really thinking about doing them. What
if you were to try to explain how to do something as routine as tying your shoelaces--
especially to someone who lives where people do not wear shoes? What would you
need to tell that person about what you were going to do? Where would you begin
to explain the procedure? What steps are involved? When are you through
explaining?

Taking Notes

Brainstorm what you are going to write by trying to answer the questions we
have suggested and the many more questions you may come up with yourself in
order to do a thorough job. Observing how you or a friend ties shoelaces is a good
way of generating ideas. Save your work in a file called SHOE1, and then take a
break.

Describing the Steps

Now return to your computer and Bank Street Writer and look over your
brainstorming. Select the items that seem most useful. You may either remember
these and clear the screen, or you may erase what you do not need and then fill in
your ideas.

Testing for Accuracy

Now test out the thoroughness and accuracy of what you have written. Read
aloud what you have written to a friend, and have this friend follow your directions
to tie his own shoelaces. Notice where your directions are clear and thorough and
where they are not. Then go back to your work and fill in the gaps. Save this as
SHOE2.

A Final Check

After a break, return to your file and do a final check. Be sure that your
sentences are complete, that you have spelled words correctly, and that punctuation

separates ideas and items in a list. When you are finished, save your work as SHOE3 and make a final print.

ADDITIONAL ACTIVITIES

Examining a process such as tying shoelaces is trickier than it appears at first. Other intriguing examples of a process are putting on a jacket, pouring a glass of juice (don't forget the glass!), and packing a bookbag for school.

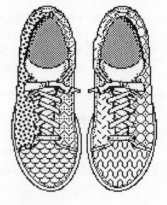

The Soap Opera

Requires: **Bank Street Write** or another wordprocessing program
          Printer

Here is where everyone in the class can get together to produce a saga using Bank Street Writer!

A soap opera is a continuous story, one in which a few crucial characters experience conflict with one another, face unforeseen obstacles, and survive (usually). The class can produce its own ongoing soap opera, but it requires careful planning.

THE PRODUCERS

A small group of students, perhaps three, can be elected by the class to

> create the list of characters
> create the setting
> set up the relationships between the characters
> write the first episode

This group of producers should save its work in a file named SOAP1. Members of the class should then read over this file and type their opinions of what the group has created at the end of the text of SOAP1. When each classmate has had a chance to critique the soap opera's beginning, the producers should consider these opinions and then make improvements. The neatest way to do this is to first erase the portions of the file SOAP1 that are no longer needed and then save the useful material as a new file, SOAP2. Remember that SOAP1 still remains intact on the data disk.

THE WRITERS

When the producers are happy with the beginning of the soap opera, then each student in the class should be scheduled to add an episode.

Establishing Guidelines

Certain rules will probably be needed to deal with those students who wish to write many more episodes than others do, for those who lose sight of what has already been written, for those who get, perhaps, too racy with their ideas, and for other problems that may arise. Once again, the producers should be responsible for setting policy on the soap opera, and the class as a whole should vote to accept its decisions.

Each episode should be saved separately on a disk, and numbered consecutively, perhaps beginning at SOAP3. Episodes can be printed out and passed around the class.

When the soap opera is complete--if it ever is--print out a final version of all the episodes. It deserves a prominent spot in the class library.

ADDITIONAL ACTIVITY

The class may want to produce their soap opera on stage for the entire school.

The Smart Kid's Guide

Requires: **Bank Street Writer** or another wordprocessing program
           Printer

All of you have to make decisions, and frequently these decisions have a price tag. If you need new jeans, you need to make a decision that will cost your family money. If you wish to play video games, you need to decide into which slots your quarters are going to go. If you are eating out, which restaurant deserves your family's hard-earned money?

You can learn a lot from other people's experiences with jeans, video games, and restaurants--and their experience can save you aggravation and dollars. To share such experiences, the class can use Bank Street Writer to set up a data bank of pooled information.

Getting Organized

Once again, there will need to be a small group to organize the project and then present its conclusions to the class for critiquing. Here is how it might work.

Suppose the class decides that it would like to produce "A Smart Kid's Guide to Video Games." Three students would be elected to set up the project. It would be their job to create SMART1 and brainstorm what exactly a kid needs to know to choose a video game--and whether they would be dealing only with arcade games, or with home games, too.

These same students would have to analyze what the features of a video game are so that their classmates would have a way of describing a game. They would also have to decide on how to evaluate how good a game is. They would share their file with class members, who might add some ideas the group had not listed. The small group would consider these items and then modify their original ideas and save them as SMART2. A paper copy of SMART2 would be posted so everyone knew what he or she had to include in an evaluation.

Pooling Information

A schedule would then be made up so that each member of the class could contribute his or her evaluation of a video game. Each new game would be saved to a new file, but those students who wished to evaluate the same game would add their work, one after the next, in the same file.

The Final Product

When each class member had had a chance, all of the files would be printed out using PRINT-FINAL.

A cover sheet could be made with the title "A Smart Kid's Guide to Video Games" and printed on the printer as it appears on the screen, but with triple spacing using Bank Street Writer's PRINT-DRAFT.

ADDITIONAL ACTIVITY

Another way of organizing this information would be to use a data base. You might consider developing another "Smart Kid's Guide" using PFS File (see Chapter 3).

Everything You Ever Wanted to Know About Widgets

Requires: **Bank Street Writer** or another wordprocessing program
Printer

Whenever a manufacturer markets a new product, you can be sure that he or she is going to let us know all about its good points to encourage us to purchase it. However, the inventor of the product, even if he or she has already spent several years getting rid of the bugs, may still feel that it is being shipped to market too soon. The happy purchasers of the new product may be surprised when they get it home--and catastrophe strikes.

The Assignment

The Widget Corporation has just shipped its new, improved widget to market. You have three assignments:

> Either alone or as a member of a small group, decide exactly what a widget is and write a commercial for the product that folks will see on television.
> Write an interview with its inventor, J. Gobs Nutsy, about the widget and how it came to be.
> Report what happened to the Smith family when they used their first widget.

Getting Started

Using Bank Street Writer as a notepad, write down your ideas of what a widget could be. You may find that your first idea is just fine, but you may also find that your fifth idea is far better. Save all of your ideas in a file named WIDGET1.

Begin a second file in which you thoroughly describe your widget: how it looks, feels, smells, sounds, tastes (whichever are appropriate). What does it do? Save this description as WIDGET2.

A Television Commercial

With WIDGET2 still in the computer's memory and on the screen for reference, brainstorm ideas for your widget television commercial. It should, of course, sell all the fantastic properties of the widget so that no one can live a happy life without it. Save your commercial in a file, WIDGET3, and clear your screen.

An Interview

Retrieve WIDGET2, which contains the description of a widget, and brainstorm ideas for an interview with its inventor, J. Gobs Nutsy. Compose this interview and save it to a file labeled WIDGET4 and clear your screen.

Reporting a Catastrophe . . . or Was It?

Finally, retrieve WIDGET2 again and brainstorm a news report of what happened to the Smith family when they used their first widget. After you have carefully written this report, save it as WIDGET5.

The Final Product

Create a cover sheet for your work, or the group's work, and print it in triple space using PRINT-DRAFT. Then use PRINT-FINAL for each of the files, WIDGET3 through WIDGET5. You now have everything you'll ever want to know about widgets.

You will notice that you have covered the same subject from three different angles. The commercial is *advertising* and always reports only good things about a product. The interview with the inventor might produce a *press release*, a public relations tool, which tells a unique story about the product also favorable to it. The story about the Smith family can be written as a *news article*, written from the point of view of an independent reporter. Which would you find the most credible?

Chapter 3

Data Base Management

Data base management--the name is enough to put anyone off! Actually, the name is descriptive of a common computer application. *Data* is factual information: For instance, the names of the children in a school are data. A *data base* is a collection of factual information organized for rapid search and retrieval. Your telephone book is a data base: By using your knowledge of the alphabet, you can quickly search and retrieve the telephone number of anyone in the book. Other typical data bases are the book catalog in the school library, the records (usually in file folders) of each of the children enrolled in the school, the list of the books a child reads in the course of the year, and your grade book.

   Data base management means maintaining and managing factual information. If you randomly type into the computer the names, classes, addresses, telephone numbers, and dates of birth of every child in a school, with data base management you can make alphabetized lists of the entire school, alphabetized lists of each class, lists by birth date for each class, and lists of the school or of each class by telephone number. Whatever is entered randomly can be retrieved in a specified order, as you decide.

AN EXAMPLE

Let's look more specifically at the list of children in the school. In the past, each child would be asked to fill in a file card that looked like this:

```
First Name: _____     Last Name: _____

Street: _____

City: _____  State: _____  Zip: _____

Telephone: _____

Birth Date: _____

Mother: _____  Father: _____

Grade: _____  Teacher: _____
```

These cards would be hand-sorted alphabetically and given to a volunteer who would type up the information in alphabetical order for distribution to faculty and families. If a list was required for each class, the cards then would be resorted and the information retyped.

Instead, let's set up a computer in the library and ask each child to come at his or her own convenience and type in this same information. The information will be entered randomly: Zake Taylor might enter his information before Mary Buchanan.

When all the children have entered their information, the librarian will ask the computer to print out an alphabetical list of all the students in the school, with their addresses, telephone numbers, and so forth. The librarian can then ask for lists of all of the children, by class. Or for the principal, a list can be created of all of the children by birthday so that each can be recognized on that very special day.

When new children are enrolled, they, too, enter their information into the computer, and new lists can be made in a matter of a few minutes.

THINGS TO REMEMBER

All data bases, whether they are the records maintained by your school, or your bank, or a student doing a research paper, follow the same procedures.

Using our list of children in a school, we can explore these procedures and their vocabulary. The list of every child in the school and all the data about them, is called a *file*. Imagine a card box with a card (like the one above) for each child. The box is the file. The card for each child is a *record*. Looking again at the card, we see that specific kinds of information are required for each child: FIRST NAME, LAST NAME, STREET, CITY, STATE, ZIP, TELEPHONE, BIRTH DATE, GRADE, TEACHER, MOTHER'S NAME, FATHER'S NAME. Each of these is called a *field*. Every data base consists of the file, the collection of all the records, and every record in the file has the same design, the same fields.

When setting up a data base, there are a few simple rules that must be followed. Because computers have no intelligence and do not know when wrong information has been entered, it is important to be accurate and to be very specific. It is equally important to be consistent. If you are entering dates of birth, for instance, they must be entered in the same way. You cannot enter January 10, 1973 for one child, Jan 10, 73 for another, and 1/10/73 for another and expect the computer to understand when you ask it to list all the children born on 1/10/73. It will only give you the records where the information matches exactly. Another example is names of states: CA and CAL and CALIF are all different to the computer.

Also, when working with data bases, it is necessary to understand that the programmers who wrote them designed each with its own specific procedures. For instance, one program might require that dates be entered as 01/10/73 and another might require the same date to be entered as 73/01/10.

In addition, all programs have their limitations. Some programs may not allow you to print your information in an order different from the way it was entered. You may be able to select a field by which you wish to sort (like LAST NAME or BIRTH DATE), but the information will always print in the order entered, from upper left to lower right.

Now let's look at a typical data base *template*. Notice that it contains the same fields as our old fashioned file card:

```
First Name:          Last Name:

Street:

City:                State:          Zip:

Telephone:

Birth Date:

Mother:              Father:

Grade:               Teacher:
```

With this template, the computer would always insist that first names have to appear before the last names in a list of everyone in the school. And grades would always have to appear before the names of teachers. So, if you asked for an alphabetized list of the names of the school children, it would look like this:

Nancy Albe
Ann Amerson
Mary Buchanan
Sheldon Moore
Zake Taylor
Anthony Zimmerman

It is important, therefore, to know the specific requirements as well as the limitations of the program with which you are working.

THE EIGHT PROJECTS

Following are eight projects that use data bases that can be useful to children and teachers alike. Project 1 is in five sections. The first section is a step-by-step description of how to set up the data base described above using PFS File. The result is a telephone book for the students in your school. The second section uses the same data to produce mailing labels. The third section creates alphabetical lists by class using PFS Report. The fourth creates the principal's birthday list using PFS Report. And the fifth creates a telephone list in a different form using PFS Report. "Classifying the Kids in the Class," Project 2, is for young children. Project 3 keeps a list of all books read throughout the year by the students in a class. Project 4 provides a method of maintaining records for a class fund raiser.

Project 5 gives students an opportunity to know who in the class has which hot album. Project 6 is a study of the history of computers. Important events in two different states are compared in Project 7. And a year-long class adventure in developing a time line is explored in Project 8.

Setting Up a School List
with PFS File

Requires: **PFS File**
            Printer

PFS (Personal Filing System) is a very useful and relatively inexpensive data base management program. It can handle about 1,000 records on a data disk. We shall use it to set up a list of all children in the school.

PFS comes in two parts: PFS File and PFS Report. We will use only PFS File for this project. PFS Report will be discussed later.

It is helpful to go through the manual that comes with the program. It is very clear, one of the best manuals available. However, for this project, you should not need to refer to the manual unless you get stuck. (Also, there is more than one version of PFS, so for more advanced functions, you should refer to the manual.)

GETTING STARTED

Set the computer up in a room that is accessible to all students, perhaps the library.

Place the PFS program in the disk drive, or in Drive 1 if you have two drives, and turn the computer on. In a few minutes, the screen will be filled with what is called the *menu*. This menu is like a menu in a restaurant. It gives you a choice of things to do.

DESIGNING A FILE

- Remove the program disk from the drive and replace it with a new disk, right out of the box. Label this disk "Students" with a felt-tipped pen.
- You will select **1** on the menu. This is DESIGN A FILE.
- Press the TAB key if you are using an Apple//e, or press the RIGHT ARROW key if you are using an Apple II or Apple II+.
    The program is now asking you for the name of the file.
- Type **STUDENTS**.
    Now hold down the CTRL (Control) key and press the C key.
    A new screen will appear. You are now being asked if you wish to DESIGN A FILE or CHANGE A DESIGN.
- Again, select **1**, and hold down the CTRL key and press the C key. (CTRL C tells the computer that you are ready to proceed. It is like using the RETURN key in many programs.)
    The computer will now show a screen that warns you that the disk in the drive is going to be overwritten, so be sure that it is the disk that you really

want to be there. The computer is now going to initialize the disk and prepare it for your data, your list of students.

- Press CTRL C.

The drive will whirr. When it has completed its task, it will present you with a screen:

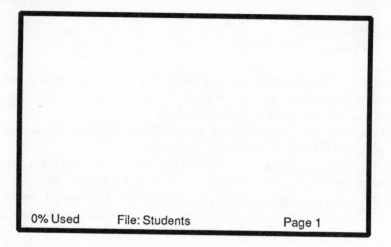

0% Used	File: Students	Page 1

It is on this screen that you will create the template for your data base. You will want to create a screen that looks like this:

```
Last Name:           First Name:
Last Name:
Street:
City:                State:          Zip:
Telephone:
Birth Date:
Mother:              Father:
Grade:               Teacher:




0% Used        File: Students          Page 1
```

In order to create your template, you will have to move around the screen. On the Apple II+, hold down the CTRL key and use the letters T, F, G, and V. You will note that they form a diamond on the keyboard. T to go up, V to go down, F to go left, and G to go right. The RETURN key will take the cursor down a line. Use the SPACE bar to make a space.

On the Apple//e, use the ARROW keys and the RETURN key to move around the screen.

- Now type in the fields (as shown above). Be sure to complete each field name with a colon (:).

The field LAST NAME appears twice on purpose. This is so that the list can eventually be printed either with the last name first or with the last name second. PFS File suffers from an inability to print in any selected order. It will only print from upper left to lower right. So, to be able to make two different kinds of lists-- SMITH SALLY and SALLY SMITH--you need to have two fields for last names.

- When you are satisfied with your template, press CTRL C.
    The drive will whirr and the menu screen will reappear.

ENTERING DATA

It is now time to start entering data.

- Select **2**, ADD, for adding data, and press CTRL C.
    The template now appears.
- Have the first child enter the information about himself. He can move the cursor from field to field using the TAB key if he is using an Apple//e. With an Apple II+, he should use the RIGHT ARROW key.

Everything should be straightforward until he gets to BIRTH DATE. If you want the computer to be able to sort by birthday, have the child leave out the year and enter the information in double integers like this: MM/DD, MM being month and DD being day. January 10, for instance, would be 01/10. March 27 would be 03/27. This is required because of the way PFS sorts.
    Also, when entering GRADE, it will be necessary to write single integer numbers as 01, 02, and 03. Otherwise the computer will later print grade 10 before grade 1. Enter kindergarten as 00.

- When all data for the first child has been entered, press CTRL C.
    The drive will whirr, and a new blank template will appear. It is now time for the second child to enter data.
- When all the children have entered their data and a final blank template appears, press the ESC (escape) key.
    This will return you to the MAIN MENU screen.

The data disk should hold between 500 and 1,000 records of this size. However, you can tell how full the disk is while entering data because the percentage used appears in a line along the bottom of the screen, below your template.

PRINTING

Now it is time to print the "School List." Once printed, it can be duplicated and sent home with the children. The list will be in alphabetical order. Each record will look like this:

> **Smith Susan**
> **6 Primrose Place**
> **Summit, NJ 07901**
> **273-9877**
> **Alice   Jim**

- In the menu, select **5**, PRINT, and press CTRL C.
- You will be asked if you wish to predefine a label. You do not. Press **2**, for PRINT, and CTRL C.
  Your template will appear on the screen.
- Press CTRL C.
  Now you will be asked some questions:

  Do you wish the Item Names (field names) **to appear?** Press **N** for no.
  How many lines per page? The default is 66. Change this to **6.**
  You will most probably have to tell the computer that you require a LINE FEED, so at that question, type **L.**

- Ignore the other questions.
- Now press **CTRL C.**
  Your template appears again.

You are now going to design the appearance of each record using + and **X**, as shown in the template below.

```
Last Name: +S          First Name: X
Last Name:
Street: X
City: +                State: +          Zip: X
Telephone: X
Birth Date:
Mother: +              Father: X
Grade:                 Teacher:


0% Used        File: Students              Page 1
```

The + tells the computer that those fields connected with a + are to be printed on the same line. The X defines the end of a line. (Fields not coded with + or X will be omitted from your printed list.) The S tells the computer that this is the field by which we want it to sort.

- Now insert the + signs and the X's, so your template looks like the one on the bottom of page 41.
- When you are finished, prepare the printer with tractor feed paper and press CTRL C.

Your list of students will now be printed out alphabetically. (To save paper, you may wish to paste up the list in several columns on one piece of paper before duplicating it for the children to take home.)

The next four sections of Project 1 use the same data base but print different reports: labels, class lists, the principal's birthday list, and an address list in a different form.

We suggest at this point that you read the manuals that come with PFS File and PFS Report. Now that you have done one exercise, you will understand the explanations with little trouble. And you will begin to understand how powerful PFS is.

Never again should a volunteer spend the summer or fall typing out the school list!

Mailing Labels
Using the "School List"

Requires: **PFS File**
         Printer

Using the data collected for the "School List," we shall now make mailing labels.

- Set up the printer with labels. Line them up so that the platen will strike near the top of the label.
- Begin with the MAIN MENU of PFS File on the screen. Place the data disk in the drive if it is not already there.
- Select **5** for PRINT.
- You do not have predefined labels, so pass through this next screen by selecting **2** and pressing CTRL C.
- When the first template appears, press CTRL C.
      We are going to print *all* of our records. We are not going to select specific sets of records, such as only one class or only those children whose birthdays are from January on. (If we had specific criteria, however, this is where we would choose them.)
- Next, you will be presented with the printing specs. You do not wish to print ITEM NAMES; press **N**.
- Lines per page are either 7 or 9, depending upon the size of your labels. If the labels are 6-line labels, then there are 7 lines per page (6 lines plus one for the space between the labels). If the labels are 8-line labels, then there are 9 lines per page.
- Remember to select **L** for LINE FEED.
- When you are satisfied, press CTRL C.
- You are presented with your second template. Select items as below:

```
Last Name:              First Name: +
Last Name: X
Street: X
City: +                 State: +          Zip: X
Telephone: X
Birth Date:
Mother: +               Father: X
Grade:                  Teacher:


0% Used        File: Students              Page 1
```

44

- Now press CTRL C to begin the printing.

If the labels are not matching up properly, press ESC to stop the computer. If your printer has memory, you may have to turn the printer off. *Do not turn off the computer*. Set up your printer with labels again and try again.

Nothing is perfect with computers. It often takes several tries to get it all together.

Class Lists
Using the "School List" Data

Require: **PFS Report**
          Printer
          Two Disk Drives

Using the same data collected for the "School List," we shall now make lists of the students by TEACHER. Instead of using PFS File, however, we shall use PFS Report. This time you will need two disk drives.

• With your computer off, place the PFS Report program disk in Drive 1. Turn the computer on.

Note for Apple users: With the Applelle or llc, you can also do a warm boot *(change programs with the computer on) by pressing the CTRL, OPEN APPLE and RESET keys simultaneously. If you are using an Apple II+, turn the computer off and then, with the PFS Report disk in Drive 1, turn the computer back on again.*

• When the MAIN MENU appears, remove the program disk. Place your data disk in Drive 1 and the PFS SortWorks disk in Drive 2. (The SortWorks disk comes with the PFS Report program and is used for sorting.) Select PRINT A REPORT.
• Again, you are printing all of your records, so pass by the first template. At the PRINT SPECS, select lines per page at **66.**
• The second template should be filled in to look like this:

```
Last Name: 2              First Name: 3
Last Name:
Street:
City:                     State:        Zip:
Telephone:  4
Birth Date:
Mother:                   Father:
Grade:                    Teacher: 1



0% Used        File: Students              Page 1
```

46

• Prepare the printer with tractor feed paper. Begin printing.

PFS Report prints in columns. The first column will be the teacher's name. The second will be the last name of each student. This list includes the student's first name and telephone number, and will be alphabetical within each class by students' last names.

A sample of what your report may look like follows:

Teacher	Last Name	First Name	Telephone
Anderson	Ambrose	James	273-0929
	Martin	Ann	277-8875
	Smith	Suzanne	522-6543
	Zachary	Thomas	273-3579
Morrow	Atherton	Rebecca	277-4286
	Carter	Megan	522-7531
	Diamond	Rachael	522-6420
	McLean	Robert	277-9645
	Thomason	Virginia	273-0246
Sinclair	Arthur	William	522-3564
	Fredericks	Mary	273-4567
	Mendham	Theodore	277-8511
	Windsor	Diana	522-0112

The Principal's Birthday List

Requires: **PFS Report**
Printer
Two Disk Drives

Using the same data collected for the "School List," we shall now make the "Principal's Birthday List" with PFS Report.
You will need two disk drives, a printer, and PFS Report.

- When the MAIN MENU appears, remove the program disk. Place your data disk in Drive 1 and the PFS SortWorks disk in Drive 2. Select PRINT A REPORT.
- Again, you are printing all of your records, so pass by the first template. At the PRINT SPECS, remember to change the P to **L**.
- The second template should be filled in to look like this:

```
Last Name: 2          First Name: 3
Last Name:
Street:
City:                 State:        Zip:
Telephone:
Birth Date: 1
Mother:               Father:
Grade:                Teacher: 4


0% Used      File: Students              Page 1
```

- Prepare the printer with tractor feed paper. Begin printing.

Address Lists--Another Form

Requires: **PFS Report**
        Printer
        Two Disk Drives

Using the same data collected for the "School List," let's now make another form of address list using PFS Report instead of PFS File.

    This list is also printed in columns. It is not as satisfactory as the original list done in Project 1a because whenever the computer comes across the same last name it will only print it once. This exercise will help you to understand the limitations of PFS Report.

    Also, only do this report if your printer is wide enough for all the columns. Your printer may only print 80 characters across the page. You will be asked for the width of your page in the PRINT SPECS. If your printer is not wide enough, you will receive a truncated report.

•   The second template should be filled in to look like this:

```
┌──────────────────────────────────────────────────────┐
│                                                        │
│                                                        │
│     Last Name: 1          First Name: 2                │
│     Last Name:                                         │
│     Street: 3                                          │
│     City: 4               State:        Zip:           │
│     Telephone: 5                                       │
│     Birth Date:                                        │
│     Mother: 7             Father: 6                    │
│     Grade:                Teacher:                     │
│                                                        │
│                                                        │
│   0% Used       File: Students           Page 1        │
└──────────────────────────────────────────────────────┘
```

•   Prepare the printer with tractor feed paper. Begin printing.

49

Classifying the Kids in the Class

Requires: **PFS File**
PFS Report
Printer
Two Disk Drives
Metric Measuring Tape and Ruler

This is a project that young children might enjoy. It could be done two or three times during the year, with comparisons recorded. The children can take home reports about themselves and write stories about themselves and the class.

Take out a metric measuring tape and ruler. This is an exercise in measuring and classifying.

The template for PFS File and Report should look like this:

```
┌────────────────────────────────────────────────────┐
│                                                      │
│    Name:                      Age:                   │
│                                                      │
│    Height:        Hair:       Eyes:                  │
│                                                      │
│    Arm:           Thumb:      Nose:                  │
│                                                      │
│    Index Finger:              Leg:                   │
│                                                      │
│    Foot:          Big Toe:    Waist:                 │
│                                                      │
│                                                      │
│    0% Used        File:Measure            Page 1     │
└────────────────────────────────────────────────────┘
```

Work in teams of three: one to be measured, one to measure, and one to type the answers into the computer. Then rotate so that each student gets to measure, be measured, and type the information into the computer.

For recording hair color, select from brown, blond, red, or black. For eyes, select from blue, green, brown, hazel, grey, or black. Everything else is a metric measurement.

When everyone has been measured, discuss how you can classify the entire class. Some suggestions are by hair color, by eye color, by height, and by length of arms. Can you find all the children who are above average in height but whose arms are shorter than average?

Finding Averages

It might help to run off reports for averages of all the measurements before attempting to classify. This will give you a starting point for classifying. To accomplish this, use PFS Report. When the second template is presented, type an A (for average) after the number designating the field order. For instance, after HEIGHT type **1A**, after ARM type **2A**, and after THUMB type **3A**, etc. This report will give you all the averages.

Classifying

When classifying, use a greater than (>) or less than (<) symbol in the desired fields at the first presentation of the template. It is at the first template that we specify the classifying criteria. For instance, for finding children who are above average in height and whose arms are shorter than average, you would type > and the average height after HEIGHT and < and the average length after ARM.

If the criterion is alphabetical rather than numeric, it must be specified by a string of characters. Specific series of letters, numbers, and spaces are *strings*. They are defined in PFS by enclosing them in double periods (..). If you are looking for all the children with brown hair, for instance, in the field HAIR, type **..BROWN..**

The computer does not read the word BROWN, it looks for the combination of characters, in this case the letters B R O W N, in that order. You could also just specify **..BR..** The computer would still find all the children with brown hair. If you used **..BL..** for BLOND, however, you would also get all the children with BLACK hair.

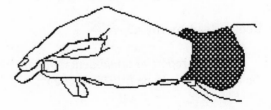

A Class Compendium of Books Read

Requires: **PFS File**
         PFS Report
         Printer
         Two Disk Drives

Using a data base management program such as PFS File and PFS Report, students and teachers can keep track of the books read by the entire class. The template might be designed to look like this:

```
Book:

Author:

Student:

Date Completed:

Number of Pages:

Comment:


0% Used            File:Books                    Page 1
```

When a student completes a book, he or she types in the pertinent information. Periodically, then, lists can be made of all books read by an individual student or by the whole class. Remember that from 500 to 1,000 records fit on a disk.

Using PFS Report, lists can be compiled by author, by book, by student, or by date read. The computer will total the number of pages read or will average them. It will count the number of books read. It will produce lists by completion dates.

Books Read by the Class

To get a report of all students, the number of books read, plus the total pages, the template would be filled in like this:

```
Book: 2C

Author:

Student: 1

Date Completed:

Number of Pages: 3T

Comment:

0% Used          File:Books              Page 1
```

The **1** after STUDENT tells the computer that this is the first field by which to sort. The **2C** after BOOK states that this is the second field and that the books are to be counted. The **3T** after NUMBER OF PAGES states that this is the third field and that a total is desired.

What Should I Read?

A list of books alphabetized by author with comments written by the students would be a helpful tool for children asking the question, "What should I read?"

```
Book: 2

Author: 1

Student:

Date Completed:

Number of Pages:

Comment: 3

0% Used          File:Books              Page 1
```

The **1** after AUTHOR designates this as the first field. The **2** after BOOK designates this as the second field. The **3** after COMMENT makes this the third field. This will give you a report, by author, of books and the students' own comments.

Retrieving a List for One Student

One of your students is moving away in mid-year and wants a list of all the books she has read during the year. Using PFS Report, at the first presentation of the template, she types her name in a manner consistent with the way she always enters it. At the PRINT SPECS menu, she can title the report (for instance, "Susan's Books Read in Fourth Grade"). Then she proceeds to the second template where she tells the computer which fields she wants printed and where she wants counts and totals. She will have a lovely report to give to her new teacher.

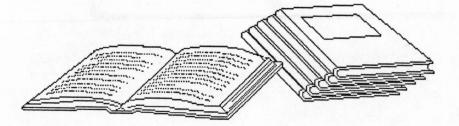

Maintaining Records for a Fund Raiser

Requires: **PFS File**
PFS Report
Printer
Two Disk Drives

The cost of class trips is increasing at the same time that school systems are getting tighter budgets. Instead of depriving the students of a worthwhile learning experience, have a fund raiser to raise the money needed for the trip and at the same time let the students manage the data on the computer.

Let's Have a Candy Sale!

Each candy bar--the large kind--costs $.50. The class will sell them for $1.00, realizing a profit of $.50 per candy bar. Initially, distribute ten candy bars to each student. Most students will sell their bars and come back for more, but there are always a few who will return some. Below is a sample template for keeping track of each student's bars.

```
First Name:
Last Name:

Bars Taken:          Bars Returned:
Bars Sold:

Profit for Class:




0% Used         File: Candy              Page 1
```

Have the students put in their own names but assign a student (perhaps the class treasurer) to help keep track of the money handed in and the returned candy. All students should watch as their records are updated to be sure they are accurate. Or if preferred, they could input their own data while the treasurer looks on.

A periodic report, using PFS Report, can be printed out and posted to indicate who is making the largest profit for the class and how close you are to your goal. This might encourage everyone to work harder.

A Record Album Collection

Requires: **PFS File**
PFS Report
Printer
Two Disk Drives

Everyone enjoys music, but it's young people who keep the record industry alive. Many of your students probably collect albums or cassettes of their favorite artists. They might enjoy keeping track of their collection, especially as part of a data base with a lot of other collections.

Students can sort their own albums by title or by artist. Or they could sort the collections of the entire class. How many students have one or more albums by Michael Jackson? Or by Men at Work? How many have the sound track for *Annie*?

Students might want to trade or borrow from each other. If there is a school dance, students can find out who has the music they want played.

Here's a simple template that will help you get started on preparing a complete list of albums in your class or school, a list that students can manipulate for their own purposes.

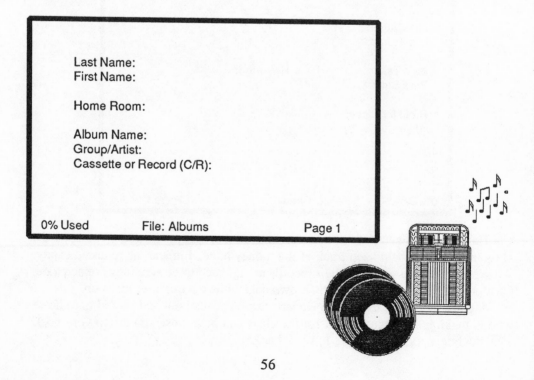

Last Name:
First Name:

Home Room:

Album Name:
Group/Artist:
Cassette or Record (C/R):

0% Used   File: Albums   Page 1

A Study of the History of Computers

Requires: **PFS File**
  PFS Report
  Printer
  Two Disk Drives

A part of every school's curriculum on computers should include the history of computers. Students can use a data base management program to collect their data and develop a report that combines all of their research. Develop templates using PFS File.

People in Computer History

History usually begins with people. Here are some names to investigate:

Pascal	Hahn	Von Neumann	Mauchly
Jacquard	Babbage	Wozniak	Bardeen
Atanasoff	Hollerith	Hopper	Eckert
Watson	Aiken	Gates	Brattain
Countess of Lovelace	Berry	Cray	Amdahl

The teacher might assign each student a person to study. As students work, they are to record as many important events from the life of their assigned person as they can. Students might use three-by-five cards to jot down their discoveries as they are working and then use assigned computer time to record their findings.

When everyone has finished, use PFS Report to create a final class study of computers. The assignments will have been recorded by person, but the report might be organized by the dates of important events.

```
Date:
Person:
Event:


Significance:




Reporter:            Source:


0% Used        File: Computers            Page 1
```

In the suggested template above, DATE refers to the date of an event, PERSON to the most important person involved in that event itself. SIGNIFICANCE refers to the reason the event is important. REPORTER is the student. SOURCE is the book, magazine, newspaper, or other source of the information.

Key Words in Computer History

Another way to study the history of computers is by key words, such as:

Abacus	Bulletin Board	IBM
ALGOL	Byte	LISP
Algorithm	COBOL	Machine Language
Analytical Machine	CODASYL	Mainframes
ANSI	Constrol Data	Microcomputers
APL	Core	Minicomputers
Apple	CRT	MIPS
Arrays	Data	PASCAL
Artificial Intelligence	Disk	Peripherals
ASCII	EBCDIC	Program
Assembler	EDVAC	RAM
BASIC	ENIAC	ROM
Binary	FORTRAN	Trojan Horse
Bit	GIGO	UNIVAC
Bug	HIPO	

The template might look like the one below. KEY WORD is the word assigned. DATE is the date of its significance. DEFINITION is what the word means. SIGNIFICANCE is why the word is important. REPORTER is the student, and SOURCE is the place the information was found.

Each student takes a key word to read up on. When all the research is completed, again compile a report by date. This will create a compilation of all the work done by the class. Each student can then discuss his or her contribution.

```
Key Word:              Date:
Definition:

Significance:




Reporter:              Source:

0% Used       File: Computers              Page 1
```

A Comparison of Events in Two States

Requires: **PFS File**
PFS Report
Printer
Two Disk Drives

We grow up knowing a great deal about our own state and the states around us. But if we live in the East, we have little feeling for the history of the western states. And if we grow up in the West, we know very little about the East. A great deal of fuss is made, for instance, about the Pilgrims landing in Plymouth, Massachusetts, in 1620. But, did you know that the Spanish settled in New Mexico in 1598 and in Florida in 1565?

It would be interesting to compare events in two parts of the country to see what was happening in one while something else was happening elsewhere. We can learn a great deal about the history of our own part of the country as well as that of another by comparing events in two states.

Selecting States

Select a state that is far away from where you live. If you live in California, select Maine or perhaps North Carolina. If you live in New Jersey, choose Washington or Colorado. If you live in Delaware, perhaps you might select Alaska. If you live in Minnesota, you might choose Florida or Hawaii.

Once you have selected a state, go to an encyclopedia and get the volumes that deal with your two states.

Designing the Template

At the computer, create a file called STATES and design the following template:

```
State:                          Date:

Event:


Comments:




Source:


0% Used          File: States                    Page 1
```

Exploring

Now, fill in the important dates for one state and then the other. It doesn't matter in what order the information is typed. At first you'll probably take the information from a table in the encyclopedia. But as you look at the information further and read about some of the events, you might find others that you would like to include in your data base.

When your data base is complete, it is time to create a list of your data sorted by date. Using PFS Report, tell the computer, at the second presentation of the template, how you want your report to appear.

```
State: 2                        Date: 1

Event: 3


Comments:




Source:


0% Used          File: States                    Page 1
```

When your report has been printed out, you will be able to compare events in two different states. You may find some surprises. We hope so.

Developing a Time Line

Requires: **PFS File**
PFS Report
Printer
Two Disk Drives

History is not dates. History is stories: stories about events, people, trends, beliefs, discoveries, inventions, wars. All dates do is place this information into one perspective--a time line. For instance, while western Europe was suffering through the Dark Ages, the culture of China was flourishing in the golden age of the Tang dynasty. While the peoples of Europe were throwing off the yoke of serfdom, the peasants of Russia were beginning to experience it for the first time.

This project is for the whole class throughout an entire year.

Each student might take responsibility for a country or topic. Countries would be selected from all the countries in the world. Topics might include explorers, important events in all the major religions, inventions, and great leaders.

Using encyclopedias and other reference books, as well as regular reading, all important dates should be jotted down and added periodically to the data base. Each student should be responsible for entering perhaps 40 to 50 dates into the data base during the year. (Remember that a PFS data disk can hold about 1,000 records, so if there is a great deal of enthusiasm, it might be necessary to create two data disks, one for dates before 1500 and one for dates after 1500.)

The template might be designed like this:

```
Date:

Country:

Significance:




0% Used              File: TimeLine              Page 1
```

DATE is the important date, COUNTRY, the country where the event took place, and SIGNIFICANCE, the event and the reason it is important.

When a report is generated using PFS Report, DATE is field 1, COUNTRY, field 2, and SIGNIFICANCE, field 3.

Periodically during the research period, ask the computer to print out a time line. This will be a very useful tool for better understanding the events and their influences upon world history. The class will begin to visualize how different cultures and trends developed side by side, sometimes affecting each other, and sometimes developing independently.

At the end of the year, print out a completed time line. It should provide the stimulus for several hours of valuable classroom discussion.

Chapter 4

Spreadsheets

A *spreadsheet* is a very powerful calculator. It allows the user to enter and manipulate a great deal of mathematical information. Spreadsheets are used in business to develop budgets, to do financial modeling, to repeat tedious arithmetic chores, and to answer "what-if" mathematical questions.

Spreadsheets as business tools are one of the most important applications for microcomputers. Businessmen and businesswomen who must work with volumes of numbers no longer use pencil and eraser or calculators. They use desk-top computers and spreadsheet programs. Students who have learned FlashCalc can make their way around Lotus 1-2-3, Symphony, or other spreadsheet programs yet to be devised, with ease. The principles are the same.

VisiCalc was the first computer spreadsheet. It was developed by two Harvard Business School students to assist them with class projects. The professor they originally shared it with said that it had no potential value. Today the two young men are millionaires. VisiCalc was the fastest selling computer program for several years and made the Apple computer an important business tool. If it had not been for Apple's success with VisiCalc, IBM would not have taken micro- computers seriously. (Lotus 1-2-3 is the most widely selling spreadsheet for the IBM PC.) Because VisiCalc is no longer marketed, we are using FlashCalc, which is VisiCalc in a new wrapper.

ELEMENTS IN A SPREADSHEET PROGRAM

Columns, Rows, and Cells

All spreadsheets look basically alike. They all have *columns* and *rows*. Letters are used to designate columns, numbers are used to designate rows. The places where rows and columns meet are called *cells*. Each cell is identified by its column letter and row number. Together, the letter and number make up its *address*. A1, B3, F16, and G20 are examples of cell addresses in FlashCalc.

To get to a particular cell, the cursor, or *cell pointer*, is used. The primary method of moving the pointer around the spreadsheet is by using the ARROW keys.

The FlashCalc spreadsheet is actually larger than what appears on the screen. Altogether, there are 65 columns across and 256 rows down, of which only 8 columns and 20 rows are displayed at any one time. You can move beyond cell H20 by using the cell pointer and the ARROW keys.

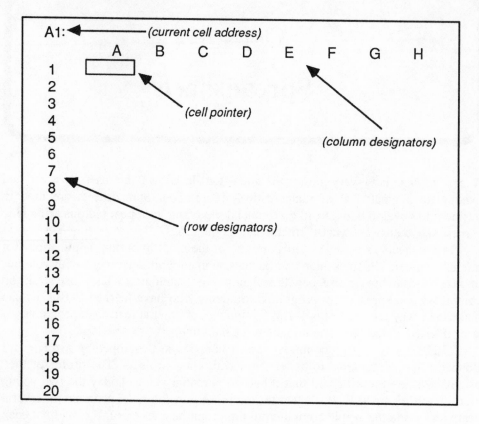

Values and Labels

There are two types of entries in FlashCalc: *values* and *labels*. Values are numeric; they can be a simple number, an arithmetic operation, or a sophisticated formula. Labels are alphanumeric; they can be words, like "Cost Per Pound," or they can be numbers that are not meant to be calculated, like the date "8/20/88." Labels are usually used as titles for columns and rows.

Examples of Formulas

FlashCalc can be used simply to record numerical data. But its real power lies in the ability it gives us to write formulas for cells that relate them to other cells and then to change the numbers in the cells. For instance, we can enter the number 7 in cell B1 and the number 5 in B2 and then tell the computer that B3 is equal to +B1+B2. If we then change the number in cell B2 to 14, the sum 12 in B3 will be immediately recalculated and displayed as 21.

That was an easy one. Say we wanted to add a really long list of numbers, for example, all the numbers in column B from row 1 to row 100. With FlashCalc, all we need to do is to enter the formula @SUM(B1.B100) in cell B101. This formula results in the sum, or total, of the column of numeric entries in cells B1 through B100. The sum will appear as the value in cell B101.

An example of another, more complex, function is @IF(G4<F7),.5,.10. In this function, if the value in cell G4 is less than the value in F7, then the value of the cell into which the @IF formula was entered will be .5; but if the value is more, then the value of the @IF cell will be .10. If the argument is true, then the first value is used; if the argument is not true, then the second value is used.

These and many additional functions are written into FlashCalc and other spreadsheet programs.

Command Level

FlashCalc and other spreadsheet programs also have a powerful COMMAND LEVEL. The COMMAND LEVEL is reached by pressing the SLASH key (/). (The SLASH key is also the division key.) At this level, we can insert and delete rows or columns, move groups of numbers, copy formulas, change the format of numbers (from two decimal points to none, for instance), clear the screen, blank out individual cells, and save spreadsheets onto a disk.

SPREADSHEET PROJECTS

The suggested projects all apply spreadsheet solutions to regular school activities and student problems. Project 1 might involve the whole school raising money for a charity. Students will enjoy Projects 2, 3, and 4--working with team scores, planning a muffin sale, and calculating grades. Middle-school students will enjoy the word problems dealing with time and distance in Project 5. They will also find Project 6, "Budget for a Class Trip," and Project 7, "Running the School Store," useful in planning for very real situations.

Although the first FlashCalc project is described with step-by-step instructions, this chapter is not designed to teach how to use FlashCalc or any other spreadsheet program. Teachers must use the tutorial in the manual that comes with the program for that.

The Holiday Fund

Requires: **FlashCalc** or another spreadsheet program

The school collects funds for holiday gifts for the poor for ten school days before winter vacation. Children are encouraged to earn the money they bring in. The class with the largest contribution at the end of the ten days gets a prize. This project keeps track, day by day, of the total contributions per day, the amount contributed to date by each class, and the total contributed by all students to date.

LOADING THE SPREADSHEET PROGRAM

- With the computer off, place the FlashCalc program in the disk drive.
- Turn the computer and monitor on. The ProDos copyright will appear on your screen.
- If you have an Apple II+, please look in the appendix of the manual to see how to enter information about your configuration.
       If you have an Apple//e or //c, press the ESC key.
- When the spreadsheet is on the screen, remove the program disk from the drive and put it away.
- Label a blank disk, one right out of the box, "FlashCalc Data" and then place it in the drive.
- Press the SLASH key (/).

INITIALIZING A DATA DISK

A whole set of letters will have appeared across the data line on the top of the screen. This is the COMMAND LEVEL. These letters represent many different things you can do with your spreadsheet.

- Select **S** for STORAGE. Other choices now appear on the data line.
- Select **U** for UTILITIES. Again new choices will appear.
- Select **I** for INITIALIZE and press RETURN.
- Type **Y** for YES.
- For the name of the volume (disk), type **SPREADSHEETS**, and press RETURN.
       The computer will initialize, or format, the blank disk to accept FlashCalc spreadsheets for saving. (You may store a number of spreadsheets on this one data disk.)

When initializing is completed, the disk drive light will go off.
- Hit the ESC key twice to return to the spreadsheet.

MOVING THE CELL POINTER

To enter labels and values (be they simple numbers or formulas) into the spreadsheet, you will have to move the cell pointer around. How you do it depends upon which Apple you are using.

On the Apple//e or Apple//c:
LEFT ARROW moves the cell pointer left one cell
RIGHT ARROW moves the cell pointer right one cell
UP ARROW moves the cell pointer up one cell
DOWN ARROW moves the cell pointer down one cell

On the Apple II+:
LEFT ARROW moves the cell pointer left one cell
RIGHT ARROW moves the cell pointer right one cell
CTRL Z moves the cell pointer down one cell
CTRL Q moves the cell pointer up one cell
(To use the CTRL key with another key, hold the CTRL key down and press the other key. Then quickly let go of both keys.)

On all machines, the GOTO function allows us to move to any cell in the spreadsheet in one step. The "greater than" symbol (>) is the GOTO key.

- Press **SHIFT >**. The computer will ask on the data line which cell you wish to move to.
- Type in a cell address (like M100) and press RETURN.

SETTING UP THE HOLIDAY FUND SPREADSHEET

The spreadsheet is set up with the numbers of the days, from one to ten, across the top, and the class designations along the left-hand column. Simple totals, using @SUM(cell address.cell address), are placed across the bottom and down the L column.

Entering Labels

Now you are ready to set up the Holiday Fund spreadsheet. In following these directions, always remember first to move your cell pointer to the cell in which you want to enter the labels, values, or formulas.

- In cell A1, type: **Class.**

- Across row 1, beginning in cell B1, type the total number of days, from **1** to **10**.
- In cell L1, type **Totals**.
- Leave row 2 blank.
- Down column A, type in the class designations for every class involved in the project.

L3 :												
	A	B	C	D	E	F	G	H	I	J	K	L
1	Class	1	2	3	4	5	6	7	8	9	10	Totals
2												
3	AMK											
4	PMK											
5	1A											
6	1G											
7	2C											
8	2D											
9	3T											
10	3S											
11	4P											
12	4H											
13	5S											
14	5Y											
15	6R											
16	6B											
17												
18	Totals:											
19												
20												

In cell L3, enter:
@SUM(B3.K3)

In cell B18, enter:
@SUM(B3.B16)

Entering and Replicating Formulas

- In cell B18, type the formula **@SUM(B3.B16)**. Make sure you type the period (.) between B3 and B16. (Note that FlashCalc shows three periods, even though you have typed only one, to suggest a range of numbers.)
- Press RETURN.

Now we are going to adapt and copy, or *replicate*, that formula across for days 2 through 10.

- Press the SLASH key (/), and **R** for REPLICATE.
  The cell pointer is in cell B18. That is the cell range we wish to copy from.
- Press RETURN.
  Now the computer is asking where we wish to copy that formula to. Our

answer is cells C18 through K18.

- Type **C18.K18**--make sure you type the period.
- Press RETURN.

The computer will now ask you if the cells are to be RELATIVE or NO CHANGE. They are to be RELATIVE (that is, the formula you want copied to column C is to refer to C3 through C16, the one copied to column D is to refer to D3 through D16, and so forth).

- Press **R**. You will be asked to press **R** twice.

Zeros will appear across row 18. This is because no data has been entered, so the spreadsheet displays totals, or sums, of zero.

- Now bring your cell cursor to L3 to enter another formula. Type **@SUM(B3.K3)**--make sure you type the period.
- Press RETURN.

Again, we will copy, or replicate, this formula:

- With your cursor in cell L3, press the SLASH key (/).
- Press **R** for REPLICATE.
- L3 is the cell in which the formula you wish to copy resides, so press RETURN.
- We want this formula copied to the cells from L4 through L18, so type **L4.L18**--make sure you type the period.
- Press RETURN.

You will again be asked if the cell addresses are RELATIVE or NO CHANGE.

- Type **R** twice.

Now, we have a formula in cell L17, when we really want a blank cell. In order to BLANK this cell:

- Bring your cell pointer to cell L17 and type **/B**.
- Press RETURN, and the cell will be blank.

ENTERING DATA

Your spreadsheet is now ready for you to start entering the amounts of money collected each day. At this point, enter the amounts with two decimal places: 1.21 or .53, for example.

At the end of each day's collection, you will be able to see the totals for each class to date, the totals collected each day, and the grand total collected so far.

Before continuing with the next projects, please study the FlashCalc manual so you can use its full power.

Team Scores

Requires: **FlashCalc** or another spreadsheet program
          Sports section from local newspaper

Young people like to keep track of the players on their favorite baseball or other
sports team. Each week, most newspapers print the records of the major league,
college, and high school teams. This spreadsheet keeps track of each player's times
at bat, hits, home runs (HR), runs batted in (RBI), and batting average (AVG). It
also keeps the team total for each record.

SETTING UP YOUR SPREADSHEET

Set up your spreadsheet as shown in the example below.

F2:						
	A	B	C	D	E	F	G
1	Player	At Bat	Hits	HR	RBI	AVG	
2	Sacks	292	88	7	45	☐	
3	Jones	232	103	9	58	.444	
4						ERROR	
5						ERROR	
6							
7							
8							
9							
10							
11							
12							
13							
14							
15							
16							
17							
18							
19	Totals:						
20	Average:						

*Formulas to enter (the numbers
and letters before the colon
are the cell addresses):*

F2: +C2/B2
B19: @SUM(B2.B18)
B20: @AVERAGE(B2.B18)

The labels for each kind of record you're analyzing go across the top on row 1.
Enter the name of each player in column A. In cell A19, enter the label **Totals**

and in cell A20, enter the label **Average**. Enter the values taken from the newspaper in columns B to E for the first player.

ENTERING FORMULAS

Column F, AVG, uses the number of hits (column C) divided by the number of times at bat (column B).

- Move the pointer to cell F2 and type +C2/B2. (The SLASH is the division sign.)
- To copy this formula for a whole screen full of players, keep the pointer on F2 and press **/R** for REPLICATE.
- The pointer is in the cell we want to replicate, so press RETURN.
- Now type where you want to copy the formula, **F3.F20**, and press RETURN.

Errors

The program will print ERROR if rows are missing data. ERROR indicates an arithmetic mistake, in this case division by 0. It will be replaced with an average as soon as data is entered in those rows.

- To BLANK cell F19, type /B and press RETURN.
- Now proceed to enter the data for the rest of the players, and the error signs will disappear.
- Another formula provides the totals of all the team players using the @SUM function. In cell B20, type **@SUM(B2.B18)**.
- You can also get team averages using the @AVERAGE function. In cell B21, type **@AVERAGE(B2.B18)**.
- Both the @SUM and @AVERAGE functions can be copied across the screen using REPLICATE, /R.

ADDITIONAL ACTIVITIES--OTHER SPORTS

This program could be changed to fit any sport. In football, keep track of yards gained, times carried, and average gain per carry for a favorite halfback. In basketball, keep track of the shots attempted, shots made, foul shots attempted and made, and rebounds of a favorite player. For team records, keep track of the standings of teams in any sport.

A Muffin Sale

Requires: **FlashCalc** or another spreadsheet program

School children are always running sales--sales to raise funds for class trips, sales for special equipment for the school, sales to help others. Our sale is to raise funds for refurbishing the Statue of Liberty. There are many decisions that must be made when running a sale. What is the product? How will we get the product? What price should we charge to make a profit? How will we market our product? To whom?

We have decided that we will sell blueberry muffins. We must determine how much of each ingredient we will need to produce the number of muffins we believe we can sell.

Ingredients for 30 Blueberry Muffins*

    1 3/4 cups all-purpose flour
    3/4 teaspoon salt
    1/3 cup sugar
    2 teaspoons baking powder
    2 eggs
    1/4 cup melted butter
    3/4 cup milk
    1 cup fresh blueberries
    1 teaspoon grated orange rind

HOW MUCH DO WE NEED?

The assignment is to design a spreadsheet that will tell us how much of each ingredient we will need for any number of muffins. That is, if it is determined that 750 muffins can be sold, how much flour, butter, sugar, and milk will we need? Or how much if it is decided we can only sell 460?

Using a spreadsheet, we can change the amounts very quickly.

---

* From *The Joy of Cooking*, Irma S. Rombauer and Marion Rombauer Becker, The Bobbs-Merrill Company, 1964.

```
E6:
            A        B     C     D   E       F
1    Muffin Sale
2    Number of Muffins:
3
4    Ingredients: Required for 30: Required for #:
5
6    Flour          1.75  cups        ┌─────────┐
7    Salt            .75  teaspoon    └─────────┘
8    Sugar           .33  cup
9    Baking Powder  2.00  teaspoon
10   Eggs           2
11   Butter          .25  cup
12   Milk            .75  cup
13   Blueberries    1.00  cup
14   Orange Rind    1.00  teaspoon
15
16                              ┌──────────────────────┐
17                              │   E6: (+B6/30)*C2     │
18                              └──────────────────────┘
19
20
```

WHAT WILL IT COST?

With the last spreadsheet we determined how much of each ingredient we would need for different numbers of blueberry muffins to be sold. The next part of our project is more complex. We need to add to our spreadsheet to determine how much each muffin costs to produce.

We will need to know what the ingredients are selling for at the local supermarket. This will require a trip to the store. We must also determine how much of each ingredient is in each package. For instance, how many cups of sugar are in a five-pound bag of sugar?

To help, the following measurements might be useful: it takes about 2 cups of butter or granulated sugar to make a pound; 4 cups of flour make about a pound; 4 cups of milk make a quart. There are 4 quarts in a gallon. There are 48 teaspoons in a cup.

Therefore, in a five-pound bag of flour, there are approximately 20 cups of flour. In a five-pound bag of sugar, there are approximately 10 cups of sugar.

This information will help us to determine how much a muffin will cost to produce.

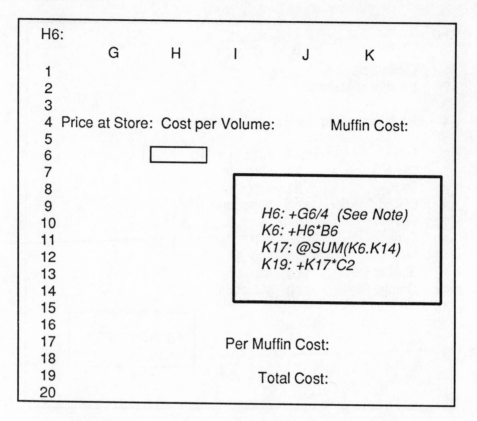

H6:

	G	H	I	J	K
1					
2					
3					
4	Price at Store:	Cost per Volume:			Muffin Cost:
5					
6		[ ]			
7					
8					
9					
10					
11					
12					
13					
14					
15					
16					
17				Per Muffin Cost:	
18					
19				Total Cost:	
20					

H6: +G6/4 (See Note)
K6: +H6*B6
K17: @SUM(K6.K14)
K19: +K17*C2

Note: The "4" represents 4 cups to a pound. If you are buying one-pound bags of flour, the correct entry is 4. If you are buying five-pound bags, the correct entry is 20. Equivalents must be worked out for each ingredient.

Grades: Homework, Quiz, Test

Requires: **FlashCalc** or another spreadsheet program

Students enjoy keeping track of their grades. This spreadsheet includes homework, quiz, and test grades. It also assumes that quiz scores are worth more than homework and test scores are worth the most.

```
B17:
          A      B       C      D     E    F    G
   1    Date  Homework  Quiz  Test
   2
   3
   4              B17: @SUM (B2.B16)
   5              B18: @COUNT(B2.B16)
   6              B19: +B17/B18
   7              B20: +B17
   8              C20: +C17*2
   9              D20: +D17*3
  10              E20: @SUM(B20.D20)
  11              F20: +B18+(C18*2)+(D18*3)
  12              G20: +E20/F20
  13
  14
  15
  16
  17   Total:   [        ]                  Average:
  18   Number:
  19   Average:
  20   Weight :
```

- Row 1 and column A are just labels and values. Type in the labels in row 1 and the labels in cells A17 through A20. And, type in the word **Average** in G17.
- In cell B17, type **@SUM(B2.B16)**. This will add all the cells in the B column from row 2 to row 16. Use the same function in cells C17 and D17: **@SUM(C2.C16)**, **@SUM(D2.D16)**.
- Move the pointer to cell B18 and type **@COUNT(B2.B16)**. This will count the number of assignments entered. Do the same for cells C18 and D18.

- Move the pointer to cell B19 and type **+B17/B18**. The average of all of your scores in column B from row 2 to row 16 will be displayed in B19. Repeat this operation in cells C19 and D19.
- The cells B20, C20, and D20 show the weighted total points for each column. Test scores were given a weight of 3 (most important), quiz scores a weight of 2, and homework a weight of 1 (least important). In cell B20 type **+B17**. In cell C20, type **+C17*2**, and in cell D20, type **+D17*3**.
- In cell E20, type **@SUM(B20.D20)**. This is the total number of weighted points. In cell F20 type **+B18+(C18*2)+(D18*3)**. This is the total number of weighted assignments entered.
- In cell G20, type **+E20/F20**. This is your overall average.

Now you can know exactly where you stand at any time of the marking period. No more surprises!

Some Math Teasers

Requires: **FlashCalc** or another spreadsheet program

TEASER 1: HOW LONG TO GET THERE?

When the West was settled, most of the settlers walked across the plains and over the mountains. Keeping a steady pace, a person can cover about 2 to 3 miles an hour and, with appropriate rests, can walk for about 8 hours a day.

For centuries, people have quickened their travel speed with horses. At a gentle canter, a horse can travel about 10 to 12 miles per hour. With appropriate stops for rest and water, a horse can travel about 6 hours a day.

In more recent years, horses have been replaced by automobiles. The legal speed limit in the United States is 55 miles per hour. With 15-minute stops every 2 hours, a person can drive an automobile for about 8 hours a day.

A Boeing 747B aircraft can travel at 625 miles per hour. Without strong headwinds, a long-distance Boeing can travel from Los Angeles to Sydney, Australia (a distance of 7,499 miles) in 12 hours. With head winds, the plane must stop in Fiji for refueling.

You are to set up a spreadsheet, using FlashCalc, that will show the differences in the length of time it would take to travel from city to city by these four different methods.

- In cell A1, type **Distance.** Cell B1 is where you will type in the distances to be traveled from city to city.
- Across row 3, the headings should be **Method, MPH** (Miles per Hour), **HPD** (Hours per Day), **MPD** (Miles per Day), **Days** (Number of Days). Enter the four methods of travel under column A and enter the data for miles per hour (column B) and hours per day (column C).
- Now, develop formulas that show the relationships between the numbers. Enter these in columns D and E.
- Remember that the actual distance to be traveled for each of the routes will always be entered in cell B1. Here are some distances to get you started:

Atlanta to Boston: 946 miles   New York to Minneapolis: 1,028 miles
Buffalo to Chicago: 473 miles   New York to Los Angeles: 2,475 miles
Seattle to Boston: 2,496 miles   San Francisco to Atlanta: 2,139 miles

Look up other distances in an encyclopedia and try them, too.

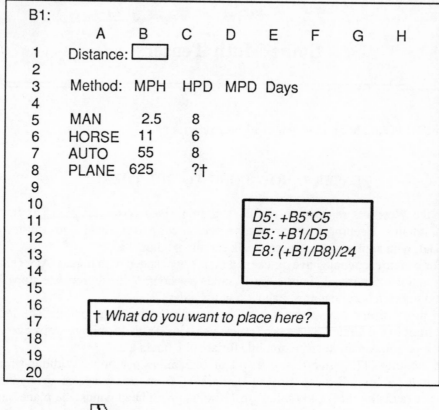

B1:

	A	B	C	D	E	F	G	H
1	Distance:							
2								
3	Method:	MPH	HPD	MPD	Days			
4								
5	MAN	2.5	8					
6	HORSE	11	6					
7	AUTO	55	8					
8	PLANE	625	?†					

D5: +B5*C5
E5: +B1/D5
E8: (+B1/B8)/24

† What do you want to place here?

TEASER 2: DISTANCE TO THE STARS

The light from the Sun takes 8 minutes and 20 seconds to reach the Earth. Light travels at a speed of 186,282 miles per second. With some simple calculation, you can easily determine the distance between the Earth and the Sun.

However, it becomes a bit more difficult to determine the distance between the Earth and Altair, which is 16 light years away. A *light year* is the distance light travels in a year.

- Set up a spreadsheet like the one below that shows the number of miles each of the stars are from the Earth.
- Also, determine how long it would take to get to each star traveling at 2000 miles per hour.

  Hint: You must first determine how many miles light travels in one year. How many seconds are there in one year?

D2:

	A	B	C	D	E	F	G	H
1	Speed of Light			186282				
2	Sun From Earth			☐				
3	Seconds in a Year							
4	Light Year							
5								
6	Stars:			Light Years:			Miles from Earth:	
7	ALPHA CENTAURI			4.3				
8	VEGA			26.0				
9	ALTAIR			16.0				
10	BETA CRUCIS			490.0				
11								
12								
13								
14				*D2: +D1*((8*60)+20)*				
15				*D3: 60*60*24*365*				
16				*D4: +D3*D1*				
17				*G7: +D4*D7*				
18								
19								
20								

Exponential Numbers

The numbers in this project are so large that the spreadsheet will show them in a form you may not have seen before, as *exponential numbers*. An exponential number is written as follows: 12.4567E+16

To write this number in a normal fashion, count to the right from the decimal point sixteen places. Rewritten, it would look like this: 124,567,000,000,000,000.

Another exponential number is 32.876E-5. This number is also written as .00032876. The minus sign tells us to count five places to the left of the decimal point. This is also called *scientific notation*.

There is not enough space in the cell for the computer to place a number that may have as many as 20 characters. Therefore, the spreadsheet will display it as an exponential number. To see the numbers in a normal way, it is necessary to enlarge the column width of the spreadsheet. Use / for COMMAND, G for GLOBAL, and C for COLUMN WIDTH. Try a column width of 17. For some of the stars, it may need to be 20 or so. Your column width can be as great as 39.

TEASER 3: HOW LONG AT SEA?

When Jason and his band of Argonauts set out to find the Golden Fleece, they could row at approximately 3 miles per hour, covering 30 to 35 miles per day. The *Constitution*, with 42,710 square feet of sail, traveled approximately 13.5 knots per hour during the years she was commissioned as a Navy fighting frigate, from 1797 through 1881.

Today, you are the captain of a freighter that travels 25 knots per hour. It is your job to carry goods from port to port around the world. You have just received orders to take cargo from New York to London (Southampton). From there, you are to continue to Lima, Madrid, Wellington (New Zealand), Tokyo, Honolulu, Cape Town, Rio de Janeiro, Paris (Le Havre), Panama City, and finally back to New York. Your ship can travel 24 hours per day. In addition to the days at sea, you must plan on 3 days (72 hours) in every port.

- Set up a spreadsheet like the one below that shows the statute miles between cities.
- Now enter formulas that will show you how long the journey will take. To do this you have to know the following:

    Nautical Mile = 1.150779 statute miles
    Knot = 1 nautical mile per hour

A1:					
	A	B	C	D	E
1	Trip:			Statute Miles:	Naut :
2	Cape Town to Rio			3788	
3	Panama to NYC			2199	
4	London to Lima			6302	
5	Rio to Paris			5692	
6	NYC to London			3452	
7	Lima to Madrid			5916	
8	Panama to Paris			5384	
9	Tokyo to Honolulu			3854	
10	Stockholm to Sydney			9616	
11	Wellington to Madrid			11086	
12	Honolulu to Cape Town			10908	
13	Wellington to Tokyo			5737	
14					
15	Distance Traveled:			E2: 1.150779*D2	
16				D15: +E6+E4+E7+E11+E13	
17	Days at Sea:			+E9+E12+E2+E5+E8	
18				+E3	
19	Total Trip:			D17: (+D15/25)/24	
20				D19: +D17+(12*3)	

Budget for a Class Trip

Requires: **FlashCalc** or another spreadsheet program

Your class has decided to visit your state capital, and you need to determine how much it will cost per person. You plan to go by bus, visit the sights, spend the night in a hotel, and return home late the following evening. You will have expenses: the bus, meals, hotel costs, and the cost of admission to the adventure park you plan to visit during your one night in town.

```
B5:
            A           B     C    D    E    F    G
  1   Participants:     43
  2   Chaperones:        5
  3
  4   Bus:          300.00
  5   Hotel:        [        ]
  6   Park Admis:
  7   Breakfast:
  8   Lunch :
  9   Dinner :
 10
 11   Total :                    ┌─────────────────────────┐
 12   Total per :                │ B5: (B1+B2)*30          │
 13                              │ B6: (B1+B2)*10          │
 14                              │ B7: (B1+B2)*4.5         │
 15                              │ B8: ((B1+B2)*6.50)*2    │
 16                              │ B9: (B1+B2)*11.50       │
 17                              │ B11: @SUM(B4.B9)        │
 18                              │ B12: +B11/B1            │
 19                              └─────────────────────────┘
 20
```

How much will the bus cost? What is the cost per person for a double room? How many meals will you be eating, and how much will each cost? What is the park admission per person? Is there a special group rate? Will there be other costs?

If this were a real trip, you would have to call the bus company. You might call several to get the lowest bid. You would call the hotel for room rates and copies of their menus. (You might plan to order the same thing for everyone for the main meals.) You would call the adventure park for rates. However, we will give you costs for your trip.

Bus: $150 each way
Hotel: $30 per person, double occupancy
Park Admission: $10 per person, group rate (regular rate, $12.50)
Breakfast: $4.50
Lunch: $6.50
Dinner: $11.50

There are 43 students in your class, and you will have five chaperones.

Are there any other expenses? What about the costs for your chaperones? Their expenses will be paid for by the students. You will have to include these costs in your calculations. Are there any others?

Will any of the chaperones and students share a room? Can you put three or four students in one room? The answers to these questions will have an effect on the total cost per student.

Running the School Store

Requires: **FlashCalc** or another spreadsheet program

Most schools have stores where they sell everyday necessities such as pencils, pens, and paper as well as special items such as decals, T-shirts, and pennants. Keeping track of inventory and profits is an important but time-consuming assignment. With a spreadsheet program, the tedious tasks can be made much easier.

To begin, make a list of everything sold in the school store. Count how many of each you have. With the T-shirts, count how many you have in each size. Find out how much each item costs. What is the price you intend to sell each item for? Now you have the information you need to set up your spreadsheet.

```
D2:
            A        B      C     D       E      F      G      H
    1     Item    Quantity Cost Value    Sold   Price  Profit
    2     Pencils              [        ]
    3     Pens
    4     Pads
    5     Decals
    6     T-Shirts
    7     Pennants
    8
    9     TOTALS:
    10
    11
    12                              D2: +B2*C2
    13                              F2: +C2*2
    14                              G2: +(E2*F2)-(E2*C2)
    15                              D9: @SUM(D2.D7)
    16                              G9: @SUM(G2.G7)
    17
    18
    19
    20
```

You will want to know what the cost of your present inventory is, how many you have sold during the month (or whatever time period you are using), how many of a particular item are still on hand, how much you have taken in, and how much profit you have made.

This is a very simple spreadsheet. You may want to know more about your stock and inventory. Design a spreadsheet that meets the needs of your school store.

Chapter 5

Graphing

Graphs are used by people in many different fields of work--from scientists, sociologists, psychologists, and demographers, to people who forecast the weather or stock prices--to demonstrate data in a visual form. A *graph* can provide a pictorial representation of complex ideas or numbers. It shows relationships, trends, and comparisons and can contribute importantly to making large amounts of information clear and concise.

Often when the conclusions of a ten-page report can be graphically displayed, the report itself becomes nothing more than a written explanation of the picture presented by the graph.

STUDENTS AND GRAPHS

Students should be exposed to graphs and charts throughout their school careers because graphing skills are an important component of expressing ideas in so many fields and professions. But students do not do enough graphing in school because creating good graphs can be a time consuming process and too often we emphasize the process of making a graph rather than the resulting message. Graphing on the computer, like wordprocessing on the computer, removes these barriers. In addition, it gives students the opportunity to experiment with the three major graph types--bar, line, and pie--so they can find the one that best tells a particular story. Even very small children can create pie graphs on a computer, something they might not otherwise do until high school.

THE PROJECTS

The projects presented here encourage students to understand what they want the results of their projects to be and how to plan and organize their activities so that they reach the desired results. Project 1 offers instructions on how to use PFS Graph, showing how to make simple bar and pie graphs.

Project 2 allows students to graph the number of books they have read over a four-month period. Project 3 is a science project in which students collect data about weights and then graph them.

Project 4 includes a series of surveys. The first is on favorite snack foods and leads to a fund-raising project. The second checks out the school cafeteria. In the third, the student body's favorite recording artist is determined, and in the fourth students have an opportunity to look into TV habits. The fifth gives students a chance to examine what they, their peers, and their families consider to be serious problems in the world and to develop some solutions. The final survey deals with a little fantasy; it includes planning a number of steps toward developing a consensus to reach a decision.

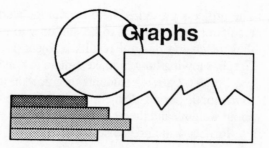

Graphs

Using PFS Graph

Requires: **PFS Graph**
    Printer with Graphics (Optional)

Before using PFS Graph for the first time, it is important to make a copy of the program. There are instructions in the beginning of the manual that tell you how to do this.

As a part of a regular school curriculum, students are introduced to graphing. Here is an example of a simple chart that you can make using PFS Graph. It has a grid, uses quantities less than ten, and is about a subject students understand.

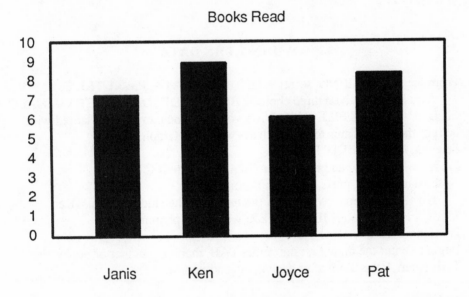

It is obvious that one student has read more books than the others. The chart tells a better story than a list: Janis 7, Ken 9, Joyce 6, Pat 8.

Displays like the one above can be created quite easily with PFS Graph, and the program also offers the user a choice of layout formats for the final product. There are essentially four steps in the process--defining the chart, entering the data for it, displaying it on the screen, and then printing it.

To many people, a graph and a chart are the same. However, in this program, the word *graph* is used to mean a pictorial representation of one data set, and the word *chart* refers to a group of graphs. The display above is a chart, and the data bar for Janis is a graph.

DEFINING A CHART

- Boot PFS Graph.

  You will see a menu that gives you a number of things you can do. Take a few minutes to look it over.
- Select **3**, DEFINE A CHART.
- Press CTRL C. (You will be pressing CTRL C when you are ready to move on to the next step. CTRL C is like RETURN in other programs.)

  Now you have a new menu. Here we are going to select the type of chart: pie, line, or bar. We will then set the legend and title for the chart. There are other selections as well, including whether you want color. You use the TAB key to move from location to location.
- At GRAPH A, under TYPE, type **BAR**.
- Under LEGEND, type **HOW MANY?**
- At CHART TITLE, type **BOOKS READ**.

  Now, you have defined the chart. It is time to enter the data.
- Press CTRL C.

PROVIDING THE DATA

- From the MAIN MENU, select **1**, GET/EDIT DATA. Press CTRL C.

  You are now given three choices: ENTER/EDIT DATA, GET VISICALC FILE, or GET PFS FILE. This shows you how you can use data stored with both of these programs to create charts with PFS Graph.
- Select **1**, ENTER/EDIT DATA.
- Press the TAB key, and type **A** for GRAPH A. Press CTRL C.
- At the data screen, press **I** at Data Format.

  Now, the program will accept the names of the students: Janis, Ken, Joyce, and Pat. **I** is for IDENTIFIER, which is alphanumeric.
- Press the TAB key.
- Begin to enter the data: first the name, TAB, then the number of books, then TAB again. Press TAB after each name and number.

JANIS	7
KEN	9
JOYCE	6
PAT	8

- When you are finished, press CTRL C to return to the MAIN MENU.

DISPLAYING THE CHART

- At the MAIN MENU, select **2**, DISPLAY CHART.
- Press CTRL C.

Voila! There is your chart.
• Press CTRL C to return to the MAIN MENU.

PRINTING THE CHART

Only printers with graphics capabilities will work with this program. To print, execute the following sequence:

• Select 6, PRINT/PLOT. Press CTRL C.
   You will be asked if you have a printer or a plotter.
• Select 1 for PRINTER. Press CTRL C.
   The program will now ask you the name of your printer. Check your manual Section 1-3 for the name of your printer.
• Select the number for the correct model, and press CTRL C.
   The printer should now print the chart.

A PIE CHART

This same data can be used to make a pie chart.

• Return to the MAIN MENU, and press 3 for DEFINE A CHART.
• Type PIE over the word BAR, and then press CTRL C.
• Now select 2 for DISPLAY CHART. You now have a pie chart that should look like this:

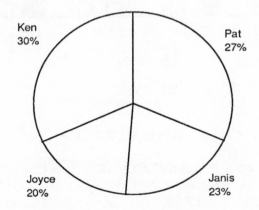

• To clear the chart from the memory of the computer, select 3 for DEFINE A CHART and at that menu, press CTRL R.

Before you continue to use PFS Graph, you might want to go through the manual that came with the program to learn about some of the other things you can do with it. You will also want to SAVE what you create on an initialized data disk.

Graphing the Number of Books Read

Requires: **PFS Graph**
Printer with Graphics

After you have been keeping track of the books that you have been reading for several months, four students should read off their totals for four months, such as from September through December. This will be a bar chart with the students' names as the legends.

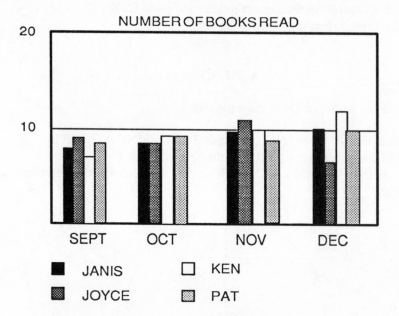

CREATING A CHART WITH MORE THAN ONE GRAPH

- Using PFS Graph, select **3**, DEFINE A CHART. Press CTRL C.
- After GRAPH A, type **BAR**. Press the TAB key. Under LEGEND type the first student's name and press TAB, TAB and type **BAR**. Continue the procedure for B, C, and D.
- For the title of the chart, type **NUMBER OF BOOKS READ**.
- Now, to enter the data for each student, press CTRL C to return to the MAIN MENU.
- Select **1**, GET/EDIT DATA. Press CTRL C.
- Select **1**, ENTER/EDIT DATA.
- Press the TAB key, and type **A** for GRAPH A. Press CTRL C.

You now have a data screen.

Remember to define the data format with an **I**. This will allow you to enter the names of the months. If you entered an **M** for Months, the computer would put them in sequence from January to December, leaving blank the months for which there was no data, and the result would be a strange graph. When typing the months, if you put **M** for March and **M** for May, the program will eliminate the **M** for March and add the two sums together.

- Type **SEPT** under X DATA, and press TAB. Type the number of books under Y DATA and press TAB.
- Do the same for Oct, Nov, and Dec. You have now computed the data for the first student.
- Press CTRL C to go back to the MAIN MENU.
- Select **1**, GET/EDIT DATA. Press CTRL C.
- Select **1**, then TAB. Select GRAPH B for the second student; press CTRL C.
  The months have already been entered, so you will only need to enter the number of books. Press CTRL C to return to the menu.
- Continue in the same manner for graphs C and D.
  You will now have a chart that shows each student's reading by months in a way that allows an easy comparison among the students.

STACKING

You can also return to DEFINE A CHART and type a **Y** after STACK. Now the total number of books read by each student will be stacked on top of each other, showing in which month the most books were read by all four students.

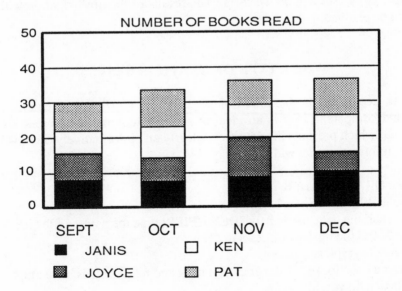

Using a Balance Scale

Requires: **PFS Graph**

COLLECTING THE DATA

Set the balance scale up in the science corner, and place 5 pencil erasers on one side. Now collect some of the following items into small containers:

pennies
crayons
pencils
paper clips
nails
screws
washers
beans

Find out how many of each of the items available are required to match the weight of the erasers. How many pencils equal the weight of the erasers? How many paper clips? How many washers? The results of this investigation will form the data to be graphed.

WHAT TYPE OF GRAPH IS BEST?

In order to decide on the best kind of presentation, two kinds of charts will be created and compared. This is an ideal project for looking at different kinds of charts to see which presents the data more clearly and informatively. First we must gather the information that will be displayed.

- Define GRAPH A as a **BAR**.
- Name it **WEIGHTS**.
- Now, enter the data, using **I** for IDENTIFIER; type the names of the items under X and the number of items under Y.
- Display the graph and save it.
- After you have looked at the graph, go back and redefine it as a pie graph.
    Which do you like better?

Conducting Surveys

Requires: PFS Graph

Surveys are a fun way to collect data for generating graphs, as well as a good way to learn what other people think. Results from surveys like the six that follow lend themselves very well to graphic presentation.

SURVEY 1: FAVORITE SNACKS

This survey is a form of market research to discover what the favorite snack ingredients are among all the students in the school so that a fund-raising project can be developed around the results.

First, have the class brainstorm and create a list of 15 to 20 different nutritious or otherwise appealing ingredients that they like in snack food. The list might include popcorn, honey, peanut butter, raisins, coconut, chocolate chips, etc.

Taking the Survey

Once the list has been compiled, send two students to other classrooms. They should read off the list to each class, asking that when they name an ingredient, students who like it should raise their hands. One student reads the list, the other counts and tallies the results.

When the surveyors have returned to their own class, the number of votes for each ingredient from all of the classes should be added together.

Graph your results.

Snack Time

Now select the five most popular ingredients. Plan a recipe for a snack that includes them all. Purchase the items. (Don't forget to use FlashCalc to work out how much of each you will need.) Make the snack and sell it to the other students in the school. The purpose: to raise funds for your computer projects.

SURVEY 2: CHECKING OUT THE CAFETERIA

There are days in school when more students bring brown bag lunches than others. Why is that? Are there certain foods that are favorites? Certain ones that are not? These questions can be answered by finding out the number of students who eat the lunch served by the school each day for a month and keeping track of what was being served each day.

Taking the Survey

Get the menu for the month from the cafeteria. Each day ask the school secretary (or the cafeteria director) for the number of students served that meal that day. When the month is completed, average any repeated entrees.

Now graph it.

What Does It Mean?

What are the favorite menus? What are the least favorite?

Should the school serve meals that are not liked by many of the students?

Can the students, working with this graphic information, make useful suggestions to the school administration?

SURVEY 3: WHO IS THE FAVORITE RECORDING ARTIST?

Everyone has a personal favorite recording artist, but who is the favorite in the class? In the school?

Getting the Data

It is very important that each student in the school vote only once, not twice or three times. Therefore, design the ballot using your wordprocessing program and duplicate just enough for the student body. Ask each homeroom teacher to distribute them for you. Completed ballots should be placed in a box outside of the school office by a determined date.

Now, have your class count the ballots.

When the results have been tallied, make a graph of the top ten.

Print out the graph and post it on a school bulletin board with a picture of the winning star.

Other Favorites

There are other kinds of favorites: record albums, school subjects, sports, favorite sports teams, hobbies, movies, TV shows, comic strips, vacation spots, etc. Choose something you would like to survey and find out how the school stands. Remember, when the results are shown graphically, they are always much more interesting and easier to comprehend.

SURVEY 4: HOW MUCH TV?

There is a lot of discussion that children today watch too much television. What is too much television? This survey will find out the number of hours of TV watched by every member of the class.

Collecting the Data

Create a form with your wordprocessing program that can be handed out to class members so they can take it home and keep track of the number of hours of TV they watch each day for a week.

When the week is over, collect the data sheets. Total the hours for each student. Now put the information into the computer. Surveys like this should not list respondents by name, so identify each student by a code or number; make the X axis the student codes and the Y axis the number of hours. The program will accept only 16 data points (that is, data for 16 students), so you may have to make several graphs.

Does the graph tell you something about the TV habits of the class?

Getting More Information

With the same data, using FlashCalc, add up the number of hours watched per day, Sunday through Saturday, and divide that number by the number of students in the class. Now graph the results. Which is the favorite night of the week? Are you surprised?

SURVEY 5: SURVEYING A PROBLEM

There are serious problems around the world. Everyone has ideas on what they are and how they can be solved. There are problems in large cities, with acid rain, with air pollution, with poverty, with starvation, and with disease.

As a class, brainstorm and select a problem. Then develop questions about that problem. For instance, if the problem was big cities, one question might be: What do you consider the biggest problem in our country's big cities today?

At dinner this evening, discuss the topic with your families. Come prepared with the single most important issue that you have decided on.

Collect these as a class. Are there one or two issues that seem to be considered the most important by many members of the class?

Create a graph that shows the ten most-listed concerns.

Taking Positive Steps

Now that you have pinpointed a problem, try to develop some solutions to the problem. Who would be involved in affecting the necessary changes? Can your class take any positive steps to make changes?

You may want to collect this information on PFS File. Then you could create a report that might be useful in your efforts. It might result in yet another graph.

SURVEY 6: ITEMS FOR A TIME CAPSULE

Your school has just received a telegram from the President of the United States in which he asks that you contribute ten items to a time capsule that is going to be buried under the Capitol steps and opened in 100 years. It is up to the students, in as democratic a way possible, to determine what your school's contributions should be.

Gathering Data

Provide each student with a ballot to write down just one item. When all the ballots have been collected, select the most common 15 items.

Now, produce a graph, print it out, and circulate it around the school, asking the students to think about what they consider to be the most appropriate ten items.

Then, pass around another ballot, asking each student to vote on ten items. You may want to use FlashCalc to calculate your results.

Produce another graph that shows the popularity of the ten selected items. This graph might be one of the items for the time capsule.

Other Ideas

Another survey of interest might be selecting items for a space capsule that is being hurled into outer space to be opened by aliens. You will need to select items that describe our world as a whole. Remember that there are weight limitations.

What about the things you would need if marooned on a deserted island? This one could probably give you a lot of laughs.

Chapter 6

Art and Music

The ultimate high-tech entertainments in the 1980s are video parlors and interstellar space war movies. They could not exist were it not for computer technology: Video games are computer programs, and space ships flying among the stars are orchestrated by computers. Since children are often fascinated by the images and sounds of video games and space movies, introducing them to art and music on the computer is an effective way to encourage the creative and artistic talents that are inherent in every child.

Some BASIC programming techniques will be introduced for creating pictures, but there is no need to fear this kind of instruction: Students who might be turned off by programs that use words and numbers will endure hours of tedious data entry to produce a picture. The challenge of creating an original masterpiece can hold the interest of students who are otherwise highly distractible.

THE PROJECTS

Project 1 introduces students to some of the BASIC graphics concepts. Project 2 instructs students how to use the Koala Pad--a good way to make use of the Apple's graphics capabilities. Project 3 introduces a program called Songwriter that allows users to write music.

A Touch of Graphics

Requires: **A BASIC Initialized Disk**
           Color Monitor (Optional)

Even the youngest children in any school setting can take advantage of the computer's graphics because there are only a few relatively simple operations to learn: defining the graphics screen, selecting colors, plotting points, and drawing horizontal and vertical lines. Once these have been mastered, they can be combined in programs to create fun and imaginative pictures.

USING THE GRAPHICS SCREEN

* Boot the initialized disk.

    You should now have a prompt. You are in BASIC. When the computer is turned on, however, it presents a TEXT screen, meaning that only characters (letters and numbers) appear on the screen. In addition to the text screen, the Apple also has several graphics screens. We shall work with the low-resolution screen, which allows us to use color.

* Type **GR**.

    This is the command that brings up the low-resolution screen. Nothing seems very different, except that the cursor is about three lines from the bottom of the screen. There are now only three lines for text. The rest of the screen is reserved for a picture.

Color

The Apple computer has 16 colors, each assigned its own numeric value, as shown below.

0 Black	4 Dark Green	8 Brown	12 Green
1 Magenta	5 Grey	9 Orange	13 Yellow
2 Dark Blue	6 Medium Blue	10 Dark Grey	14 Aqua
3 Purple	7 Light Blue	11 Pink	15 White

Color is defined in BASIC by typing **COLOR** = followed by the number of the color. Here are some examples:

COLOR = 12	(the color will be green)
COLOR = 9	(the color will be orange)

- Try out the command by typing the program line **COLOR = 6**.

    Nothing seems to happen, but everything you draw from this point on will be medium blue until you change the color.

Plotting Points

The screen of the monitor is divided into a grid that has 40 horizontal (sideways) rows and 40 vertical (up and down) columns, each numbered from 0 to 39. Any point on the grid can be located by specifying the numbers of the row and column that intersect at that point; for example 0,0 is the upper left corner, and 39,39 is the lower right corner. When the computer is given the command **PLOT** followed by the numbers that locate a point, it will place a small square at that point when RETURN is pressed.

Here is a brief exercise that will help you find your way around the screen:

- Type the following lines. (Remember to press RETURN after completing each line, and watch the screen each time you press RETURN.)

    PLOT 0,0
    PLOT 39,0
    PLOT 0,39
    PLOT 39,39

You should now have little blue squares in all four corners of your screen.

Horizontal and Vertical Lines

To draw a line on the screen, you have to tell the computer whether it is a row or a column, where to begin the line on the grid, where to end it, and in which row or column it should be placed. The commands you will use are **HLIN** (for a horizontal line) and **VLIN** (for a vertical line) followed by the numbers of the rows or columns where the line is to begin and end, and then the word **AT** and the number of the row or column in which the line is to appear. Like the PLOT commands, these command statements are activated when you press RETURN.

Here is an example of how to draw lines with the computer:

- Begin with the horizontal line by typing **HLIN 10,20 AT 30**. Press RETURN.

    You now have added to your screen a horizontal blue line located 30 points down from the top and stretching across the screen from point 10 to 20.
- Change the color of the next line to orange by typing **COLOR = 9**. Press RETURN.
- Now draw a vertical line by typing **VLIN 5,15 AT 25**. Press RETURN.

    An orange vertical line is now added to the screen, extending from point 5 to point 15 in the column 25 points from the left edge of the screen.

WRITING A PROGRAM

You could continue to draw in the *immediate mode*, where the computer reacts each time you press RETURN, but it is also possible to write a program that will draw a picture which you can then save onto the disk.

All BASIC programs require *line numbers*. These numbers tell the computer the order in which you want it to do things. For instance, a program that tells the computer what we did step by step above reads as follows:

```
100 GR
110 COLOR = 6
120 PLOT 0,0
130 PLOT 39,0
140 PLOT 0,39
150 PLOT 39,39
160 HLIN 10,20 AT 30
170 COLOR = 9
180 VLIN 5,15 AT 25
```

The computer will always do things in numerical order from 1 to infinity. It is customary to leave gaps between line numbers so that changes can be made in the instructions to the computer. Programmers traditionally leave 10 spaces between line numbers, which is why our numbers are 100, 110, 120, etc. This is to allow for additional lines to be added later. Most programs begin at number 10 or 100, but counting can begin anywhere.

A Smiling Face

Here is a program that uses all of the graphics statements:

```
NEW
100 REM SMILING FACE
110 HOME
120 GR
130 COLOR = 9
140 REM FACE FRAME
150 HLIN 10,30 AT 5
160 HLIN 10,30 AT 25
170 VLIN 5,25 AT 10
180 VLIN 5,25 AT 30
190 REM NOSE
200 PLOT 20,25
210 REM MOUTH
220 COLOR = 1
230 HLIN 15,25 AT 20
240 PLOT 15,19: PLOT 25,19
```

```
250 REM EYES
260 COLOR = 2
270 PLOT 15,10: PLOT 25,10
280 PRINT "GOOD MORNING!"
290 END
```

The program includes the following commands that you have not seen before:

NEW clears the computer memory. It is always a good idea to start the writing of every *new* program with NEW.

HOME clears the screen and places the cursor in the upper left-hand corner of the screen. It does *not* clear memory.

REM means *remark*. It is a programmer's way of describing what is going on in the program. The computer does not read remarks: it ignores them. REM is for people only.

A colon (:) completes a statement and allows more than one statement to a line.

END tells the computer that this is the end of the program.

- Try typing in this program. Remember to press RETURN after each line. When you have completed entering the program, type RUN to see the picture it creates. Remember to press RETURN.
- To save this program, leave the initialized disk in the drive and type SAVE FACE. Press RETURN.

Your Own Picture

Now it is your turn to draw your own picture.

It might be useful to use some graph paper, numbering from 0 to 39 across the top and from 0 to 39 down the side. Draw your picture on the graph paper, then plot the points on the computer. (There are only command statements for plotting points, vertical lines, and horizontal lines. If you wish to draw a diagonal line, do so by plotting each point on the line individually.)

- You can see the picture you are creating at any time during the programming process by typing RUN.
    The picture you are building will appear on the screen.
- To get out of GRAPHICS and back into TEXT mode, just type TEXT and press RETURN.

When you have a picture that you like, save it. It is a good idea to save several times while you are working on your picture. As long as it is on disk, it is quite safe, but power failures and kicked cords can cause a total loss of your work. Better "saved" than sorry.

It is also possible to make more complex pictures and to include animation. There are many books on the BASIC language that can teach you how it is done.

Using a Koala Pad

Requires: **Koala Pad**
              Color Monitor
              Printer with Graphics (Optional)

Using a Koala Pad, you can draw very intricate pictures on your computer, save them to disk, include them in other programs that you write, and print them out on a printer. To use the Koala Pad, plug its cable into the game port; it will now work like your paddles or joystick, and can be used the same way.

Before using the Koala Pad and the Illustrator disk that came with it, be sure to make several copies of the disk and place write-protect tabs on them. Be sure to have several initialized, or formatted, disks on hand to save any pictures that you create. (A picture takes up a great deal of disk space; a disk can hold only a few pictures.)

THE KOALA PAD

The Koala Pad is designed for drawing. Using the stylus that comes with it, you draw on the pad and what you draw appears on the screen of the computer. There are two buttons on the pad: they both do the same thing. Use the one that is most comfortable for you to use.

When you boot the Illustrator disk, the first thing you will see is a very colorful introductory screen. This is the copyright page. To move to the menu of the program, press one of the buttons.

THE MENU SCREEN

The Menu Screen is divided into three sections: actions, pen size and shape, and colors.

You should see a little arrow on the screen. Move your stylus across the pad and you will see the arrow move. By placing the arrow over a selection and pressing one of the buttons, you choose an action, a pen size, or a color. There are two sets of colors and you may use colors selected from both color sets in the same picture. It is best to begin by experimenting with all of the pen choices.

At the bottom of the screen, it says "RETURN TO PICTURE." Whenever you have finished making your selections and wish to move to the picture screen, bring your stylus to the bottom of the pad, thus bringing the arrow to the bottom of the screen, and press one of the buttons.

ACTIONS

Here are the things that you can do to draw your pictures:

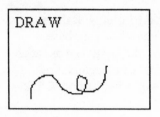

This selection allows you to draw. Click one of the Koala Pad buttons to start drawing, move the stylus around the Pad to make the desired design, and click again to end drawing.

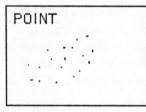

Here, to make points, click the Koala Pad button to make a point where the stylus is resting on the pad.

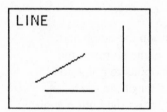

To make a straight line, point the stylus at the place where you want to make the beginning of the line and click the button; then move the stylus to where you want the end of the line and click.

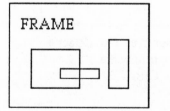

Click to define one point on the rectangle. Then move the stylus about to choose the end point of the diagonal; when satisfied with the size and shape, click again.

This is for a filled box. Select a color in advance. Then use the buttons and stylus as with FRAME.

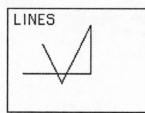

This is for connected lines. Point and click at the point where the lines are to begin. Then point and click at each joining. When you are finished, click twice.

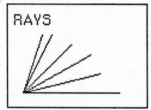

Rays are really fun. Point with the stylus to where you want your base. Click. Then move the stylus out as far as you want your ray. Click again. Now make rays until you want to stop. Click again.

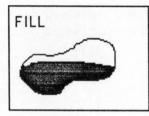

If you want to fill in certain parts of your picture, make sure that everything meets, then select FILL and a color. Return to your picture and move the FILL cursor to the desired place and click.

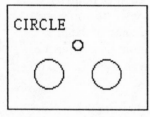

Select one point on the circle and click. Now move the stylus in the direction of the opposite point, to define the diameter of the circle. When satisfied, press the button again.

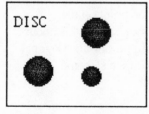

DISCS are colored circles. Select a color first, then follow the instructions for CIRCLE.

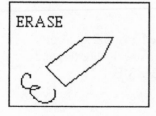

ERASE allows you to clear the screen. When you select ERASE, the program will ask SELECT COLOR TO ERASE. This is a request for a new color background. Black is a safe color. Try others.

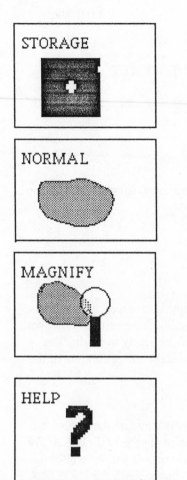

STORAGE allows you to save your picture. Be sure to have an "initialized" disk ready to save your picture on. Follow the instructions.

This allows you to see everything that you have drawn on the screen. NORMAL is only used after using MAGNIFY.

MAGNIFY is a real treat. It allows you to see your work very close up. You will see pixel by pixel, or point by point, what you are actually drawing. With color, you have lots of control.

If you are ever confused, use HELP. It will help you find your way.

SOME HINTS

When you first click to the drawing screen, you will see a black screen with nothing on it. Place your stylus on the pad and move it about. You will see your pointer.

Now draw some lines and circles and rectangles. Fill in the areas with different colors. Just get a feel for how the Koala Pad works. When you have played around, ERASE your screen and start some serious work.

Beware of FILL. If there is one little hole in the lines surrounding the space you are filling, the entire picture will be ruined.

PRINTING

Read the instructions that came with your Koala Pad for printing. If your printer can print graphics, print through STORAGE.

Getting Started with Songwriter

Requires: **Songwriter**
        (a blank initialized disk)

Songwriter is a program that allows you to create your own songs, make changes in them, and save your masterpieces on a floppy disk.

YOUR FIRST SONG

- Boot the Songwriter disk.

  As the disk boots, you will not only see the copyright screen, you will also hear a sample of the kind of music you can make using Songwriter. When you see the screen that looks like a piano keyboard, you are ready to begin. The letters and symbols around the outside edge of the screen are reminders of the things you can do.
- First push the RETURN key.

  You just played your first note.
- Now watch the screen and press the RIGHT ARROW key and then press the RETURN key. Move the note in the other direction using the LEFT ARROW key. You can also move a half step by pushing the < or > keys. Take a few minutes to move up and down the scale; after each move, push the RETURN key.

  The RETURN key will play a note as often as you like, but it will not record notes. To record notes, use the SPACE bar.
- Press the SPACE bar now.

  You have just recorded your first note. Use the arrow keys to move to new notes and press the SPACE bar after each note.
- If you would like to record a rest (a silent space), press the **0** (zero) key.
- After you have recorded several notes, press the **P** key to play them back. You now have the beginning of your first song!

LISTENING AND CHANGING

With Songwriter, there are several ways to listen to your song. Hold down the UP ARROW key. Now hold down the DOWN ARROW key. You should have heard your song played forwards and backwards. Notice that your notes move up and down the screen like the holes on a roll of player piano music. (On the Apple II+, first hold down the **N** key and the REPEAT key simultaneously. Then hold down the **V** key and the REPEAT key.)

Pressing and releasing the forward or backward play key will make the computer play the song one note at a time.

If you want to add a note to your song, use the forward and backward play keys until you reach the point where you wish to add the note. Then use the LEFT ARROW and RIGHT ARROW keys to select the note and press the SPACE bar. Now select the **P** key to listen to the change you made.

To remove a note, use the forward and backward play keys until you hear the note you wish to remove. Then press the **X** key. The last note you heard was erased. Press **P** to hear the change.

SELECTING AN OPTION

The options screen is reached by pressing the **G** key. You will see a menu. Here you can choose to initialize a disk for saving songs, save a song, start a new song, or load an already-saved song from disk.

Press **G** to see the options screen. There is now a menu. Use the RIGHT ARROW and LEFT ARROW keys to move from choice to choice. To select a choice, press the RETURN key. To get back to your song, you may either press the ESC key or select the RETURN TO SONG option and press RETURN.

When you select MAKE A NEW DISK, which is the Songwriter command that initializes a diskette, remember that the disk is going to be written over and anything on that disk will be destroyed. So be sure you use a blank disk or one that doesn't have any data that you might want again.

When you use SAVE SONG, be sure to give your song a name that will mean something to you later.

Before you use START NEW SONG, be sure that you have saved the old song; otherwise it will be erased from memory.

USING ADVANCED FEATURES

You can make your song play faster or slower by using the **F** and **S** keys. Try pressing the **F** key several times and then play your song. Try pressing the **S** key several times and then again play. A clue to fast and slow is a bouncing dot in the upper left-hand corner of the screen.

Note lengths can be changed. Look at the left side of the screen. You will see a fraction (1/8) and a set of boxes. One box out of 8 boxes is filled in. That represents the fraction. Typing in a number from 2 to 8 will change the fraction. This fraction represents the length of the note. By typing a 1, the fraction is 1/8, an *eighth note*. By typing in 8, the fraction is 8/8, or a *whole note*. You get a *half note* by typing 4, for a fraction of 4/8. To use this feature, select a length, then a note, and then press the SPACE bar.

You can multiply and divide notes. The symbols used are * for multiply and / for divide. As an example, suppose you want to change a 1/8 note to a 1/4 note.

Play forwards or backwards until you hear the note. Then press the * key followed by the **2** key. The note will change. To change a 1/4 note to an 1/8 note use the / key instead of the * key.

Every note has a name. To see the names of notes as they play, press **G**, then select NAME NOTES. Then select RETURN TO SONG. Press **P**. The names of the notes will scroll along the left side of the screen.

To print a song, press **G** and select PRINT NOTES. Follow the directions as they appear on the screen. When the song has printed, you will be returned to the regular screen.

USING THE "IDEA" CAPABILITY

An idea is a series of steps that can easily be used with different notes. The **L** and **K** keys are used to record ideas.

Press the **L** key and look for the light bulb on the screen. Record a few notes in the usual way, using the arrow keys and the SPACE bar. When you are done, press a key that Songwriter does not use, such as the **Z** key. The light bulb will disappear. Now press the **Z** key again. You will hear a sequence of notes. Use the arrow keys to move up and down the scale. Now press the **Z** key again. You will hear the same sequence but with different notes. An idea records the pattern rather than specific notes.

If you are unhappy with the idea, press the **K** key. You can remove an idea by pressing the DELETE key or return to the regular screen by pressing RETURN.

Have fun writing songs!

Chapter 7

Communications

TWENTY YEARS AGO

In 1967, the major means of business communication was the postal service. Although messengers were used for urgent deliveries in major cities like New York, most written materials were mailed. London had two deliveries daily; a letter posted in the morning was usually delivered in the afternoon. Although personal mail was usually sent by "surface," businesses were willing to spend the extra cost to send business correspondence across the country and across oceans by air.

Urgent messages to be sent long distance were usually sent by telegram or cable. A person visited or telephoned the local telegraph office and gave them the message, which they then relayed to a telegraph office at the destination. Until the 1920s, when teletypewriters came into use, all messages were sent by Morse code. Telegraph lines had been laid in much of the United States by the late 1840s and stretched from coast to coast by 1861; the first successful transoceanic telegraph cable was laid across the Atlantic Ocean in 1866. Eventually, as more cables were added to the system, telegrams could be sent almost anywhere in the world.

It was not until 1956 that the first trans-Atlantic telephone cable was laid. By 1960, it was possible to have 100 simultaneous conversations taking place on the same cable across the Atlantic. The telephone had become a common business tool, but long-distance calls were expensive and the connections were often bad. In a conversation between Paris and Houston, the person at the other end of the phone might sound almost as far away as he actually was!

Newspapers had facsimile machines that transferred pictures from one place to another. It was a slow and expensive process, but it allowed a Berlin newspaper to print a picture taken in Los Angeles. These pictures were transferred through the telegraph system.

Office copiers in most businesses were Thermofax machines. They used special paper, they were very slow, and the copy was brown on beige. For most correspondence, secretaries made carbon copies of their work as they typed.

A lawyer researching for a case in 1967 might employ as many as ten other lawyers to manually search through the volumes of case law to try to find other cases related to his own. And even after weeks of work, he would never know for sure whether he had all the "cases in point."

1987

Twenty years later, business communications had changed dramatically. Businesses rarely used the postal service even for intra-city correspondence; it was too slow. Mail no longer cost extra for air mail delivery. The telegraph system, as it was known in the 1960s, no longer existed. Long-distance telephone calls, now crystal clear and much less expensive, were relayed by satellite. Every business of size had a facsimile machine for sending not just pictures but total documents instantaneously by telephone. Every business had a duplicating machine that produced copies that looked like the original; secretaries did not make carbon copies any more. Lawyers did research by computer, no longer leafing through volumes of decisions.

A communications revolution had taken place for business by the mid-80s. However, the general public was only beginning to recognize the changes. They continued to use the postal service and to complain about it. They rarely telephoned Europe because they didn't realize it cost no more to call Hamburg than to call Houston. They made their copies at the local library. Business had changed the way it communicated--the way it did business; the public's turn was coming.

Members of the public were beginning to experience the results of the changes, mostly through their televisions. They had watched instant replays of the attempted assassination of the president of the United States and of the pope. They had watched the take-offs and landings of space shuttles, and had even viewed the events that had taken place on board. Television signals relayed by satellite made it possible to interview a Soviet official in Moscow and a U.S. official in Washington simultaneously. Millions of people had purchased video cassette recorders, and the video rental business was booming. Video games, at special video parlors, at some restaurants, and even at movie theaters, were the rage among young people and, in some cases, a community social concern. The public was being offered telephones free with magazine subscriptions. On TV, MCI, an independent telephone system, was advertising its electronic mail system.

Home computers had been heavily advertised in newspapers and on television, and many families had bought them as Christmas or birthday gifts. Often, however, setting up and using the computers seemed to be too complicated a process and many of them ended up on closet shelves. But even such setbacks could not impede the rapid transition that was taking place in society. By the mid-80s, the newest computer technology made it possible for nearly all citizens to use computers with very little instruction.

A marriage between telecommunications, television, and computers had transformed business, and these same changes were becoming an integral part of the way we all lived and did our personal business.

EXAMPLES OF THE COMMUNICATIONS REVOLUTION

A Business Conference. How does AT&T conduct a business conference when people in Los Angeles, Chicago, and New York need to talk? In the old days, they would meet in Chicago. Now they no longer travel: TV cameras are set up in each conference room, the phone lines are opened, and the meeting is held. Speakers' presentations, graphics displays, and group reactions are transmitted to all locations instanteously.

A Lawyer's Research. Using a small desk-top computer linked by telephone to a mainframe computer that contains LEXIS, a national legal data base that stores the texts of thousands of court decisions, administrative rulings, laws, and regulations, a lawyer can search for a selected phrase in every case or authority applicable to his case in about 20 minutes. He can investigate the past testimony of his opponent's "expert witnesses." He can study the decisions of the judge he may be trying a case before.

Negotiating a Sale. A businessman in Phoenix is trying to purchase a company that is headquartered in London. Communications are handled by telephone until the final negotiations. The lawyers arrive from London not with ten copies of a 100-page purchase agreement, but with three disks (two back-ups) to be printed out and copied on site. Changes are made instantaneously and incorporated into the purchase agreement throughout the negotiations until a final contract is signed.

Instant Transactions. A businesswoman in Rome dictates a letter to her secretary. The secretary types it into a computer with a modem, using one of the variety of wordprocessing programs. Through one of the electronic mail services, the letter is promptly delivered to the client in San Francisco. The client responds within minutes. A few years ago this same transaction would have taken ten days. Now it takes ten minutes. And the cost is about the same.

A Salesman's Portable Office. A salesman on the road collects his orders for the day using a small computer that fits in his briefcase. When he returns to his hotel room, he connects the computer's built-in modem to the telephone line and sends his customers' orders to a computer at his home office. He also picks up any messages that have been placed in his "mail box." Any correspondence he has developed throughout the day is printed out for him at the home office.

The Scientists' Network. A scientist at Stanford University has, for a number of years, been plugged into a Defense Department network. Each morning, she checks her computer "mail" for messages and reads them with her morning coffee.

Shopping. A community in northern New Jersey is experimenting with ordering food, clothing, and household needs through a TV and computer connection. Other electronic shopping is available through a number of services.

Experts Share. A computer teacher in Palmer, Alaska, subscribes to The Source and CompuServe. Through these services he communicates daily with other experts in the field of the language LOGO. Sitting in his study at home, he can, for the cost of a local telephone call and about $10 for an hour of time-sharing on the services, chat with his peers in Boston, read messages from a professor in Los Angeles, or send thoughts on a new idea to a fellow teacher in Toronto.

Travel Plans. Using a home computer, a family planning to fly from New Orleans to Chicago for a family reunion can contact The Source and look up all airlines flights on a specific day or within a group of days. They can completely bypass the travel agent by then calling the chosen airline directly and booking seats on the selected flight. If that flight is filled, other possible flights on the list they have printed out can be considered.

Bulletin Boards. A 12-year-old boy in New Jersey is a sysop (system operator) who runs his own BBS (bulletin board system) from his bedroom. He is one of thousands of teenagers throughout the country who have never met but communicate daily through their computers. They are known to each other by intriguing names: "The Wizard's Apprentice," "The Surgeon," "The Turk," "The Magician," "The Chief."

BRINGING THE COMMUNICATIONS REVOLUTION
TO THE CLASSROOM

All of the examples above were common practices in 1987, the beginning of a universal mass communications system. The way the students of today will communicate in the future--to send a letter, to receive a magazine, to shop for clothes--is more like the examples above than the way we do things now.

Moreover, with a modest investment in hardware and software, most of these techniques are available to students in the computer-equipped classroom. With this book in hand, the teacher can convince the administration that a few simple tools are required: a modem, preferably a Hayes micromodem; an accessible telephone line; a BBS Shell program; subscriptions to The Source and/or CompuServe; and a small budget for time-sharing.

COST CONTROL AND SECURITY

It would be extremely unwise to start up a communications system without giving serious thought to protecting it from unauthorized use. If school phone lines are used for long-distance calls to bulletin boards, the charges for these calls can become very expensive, particularly since long-distance rates are at their highest during school hours. Also, bills for connect time to The Source and CompuServe can be staggering if students have unrestricted access to the school's account. Therefore, once a school has decided to include communications in the computer curriculum, it is imperative that security arrangements be worked out before the system is put into operation.

Use of telephone lines is most readily controlled by assuring that computers connected to them are always monitored by a teacher. For additional protection, find out if the school's phone system allows long-distance access restrictions to be placed on specified extensions; if this is possible, it can make the teacher's job much easier.

Passwords are the key to controlling access to The Source and CompuServe, since passwords are required for signing on to all such services. No one wants students to run up the bill by connecting to these networks through a home computer at night; we therefore recommend that passwords be changed daily by the teacher in charge--after the students have left for the day.

These two measures are the best protection currently available and should provide the needed security. It must be stressed, however, that they must be practiced conscientiously: Neglecting to change the password one night or leaving a phone unmonitored can have very unfortunate consequences, and may jeopardize the continuing availablility of these resources.

THE COMMUNICATIONS PROJECTS

Project 1 is accessing a local computer bulletin board. Once one board is found, the students will find that there are many more. Soon, they may want to set up their own all-school board; details of how to do this are included in Project 2. Of course, the board must be maintained. This is described in Project 3.

Large data bases exist that can provide current information and the ability to chat with others from all over the world: Students are invited to explore two of these, The Source and CompuServe. Projects 4 and 5 discuss signing up and getting started on these services.

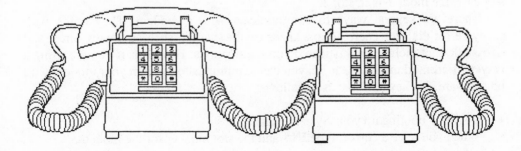

Accessing a Bulletin Board Through BASIC

Requires: **Modem**

What is a computer bulletin board system? A BBS is an electronic bulletin board, very much like a bulletin board at school or in your family kitchen. It is a place where messages from one person or organization are posted for others to read and respond to. Since the very early days of microcomputers, there have been BBSs all over the country. Some have lasted for a very long time, but most come and go with the interest of the system operator, or sysop.

FINDING THE FIRST *BBS*

Young people across the country are enchanted with BBSs, and there are probably several in your area code; it is only necessary to find one of them. (We recommend that you keep your inquiries within your area code to save money since telephone calls can become expensive.) The easiest way to find a BBS is to contact a computer enthusiast. Chances are that at least one student or teacher in your school system, or a friend of one of them, will have a BBS number. You might also try asking at one of the local computer stores. If you are really stuck, you can find help in *The Computer Phone Book*, by Mike Cane (New American Library, 1983).

Once you have signed onto a BBS, you will find that it lists other BBS telephone numbers. You will soon have a long list, and it won't be long before you have favorites.

SIGNING ON

You now have the telephone number in hand. The next step is to tell the computer to dial the number through the modem that is installed in your computer. If you are using an Apple II+, the modem is probably plugged into slot 3. If you have an Apple//e, the modem is in slot 2.

There are several ways to communicate with a modem. They come with software for dialing. There are packages on the market, such as SmartCom II and Crosstalk, that include sophisticated communications. However, if you are using a Hayes Micromodem II , //e, or //c, you can communicate through your modem with no software.The key stroking is as follows:

- Begin by booting up your System Master.
- When you have a cursor, type **IN#** and the slot number for the modem.

114

Press RETURN.
- Press **CTRL A**.
- Press **CTRL F** for full duplex. (Some communications require CTRL H, for half duplex, but that comes with more complex systems.)
- Press **CTRL A** again.
- Press **CTRL Q**.

The computer will now give you a message: MICROMODEM DIALING:
- Type in the telephone number you wish to call.

It is important to type in the number slowly to avoid mistakes, because backspacing will interrupt the dialing. You may use dashes to separate the numbers. You will be able to hear the modem dialing, if ever so faintly.

After the modem has completed dialing, you will receive the following message: MICROMODEM AWAITING CARRIER. About 30 to 60 seconds will elapse. If there is no answer at the number you called, or if it was busy, the computer message will be: NO CARRIER: HUNG UP. If you want to try again, type **CTRL A** and **CTRL Q** and reenter the telephone number.

If a connection is made, however, the message will be: CONN:

In just a few seconds, the other computer will begin transmitting to you. Read the instructions, answer any pertinent questions, and explore the various items on the *menu* (the choice of things to do).

EXPLORING THE *BBS*

Some bulletin boards will require that you join them even if you just want to chat or read the bulletin board. Others will allow you to read whatever you want, but will not permit you to leave messages until you have joined. Joining usually requires no money, although a few dollars are always welcomed to help defray the costs of the BBS. Since sysops like to know who is using their boards, they will ask for your name, address, phone number, and, of course, for your *handle*, or transmitting name. Handles are names such as "The Wizard's Apprentice," "The Executioner," "Col. Hogan," "Sweet Pea," "Tumbleweed," "The Mace," "Dungeon Master," "The Arsenal," and "Dr. Who." Be as creative as you like in choosing your handle.

Many bulletin boards will limit the amount of time you may stay on and will disconnect when you have stayed beyond your welcome. With some, the length of time you can stay on is increased the longer you have been a member and have posted bulletins. If you are lucky, the sysop will be on line and will talk to you. *(Sysops are usually not on-line during the family dinner hour!)*

Before signing off, be sure to select the menu item that gives you the telephone numbers of other BBSs. This choice might be called OTHER BBS'S. Calls to BBSs can result in your learning what other people--both young and not so young-- are doing with their computers. You can learn about meetings of computer clubs where you can make new friends, learning what they know and sharing with them what you know. In addition, many BBSs feature topics other than computers. There may be opinion polls, discussions of current events, and listings of items for sale. Many sysops have interests other than computers. Many BBSs have become like clubs, and it is important to get a feel for the members before leaping in. However, sysops want messages left on the bulletin boards, as it is messages that keep the BBS interesting to the members. Be prepared: In addition to interesting BBSs, you will also find some with many tasteless sophomoric messages posted and not deleted by the sysop--these BBSs tend to be short-lived.

Always use the log-off command designated by the BBS; it's never polite to hang up the phone abruptly. However, if you must break a connection in haste, type **CTRL Z**. This will automatically disrupt the connection and hang up the modem.

Setting Up an All-School Bulletin Board

Requires: **Modem**
ByteMaster BBS

After exploring a number of bulletin boards and chatting with their sysops, you will probably want to set up your own bulletin board. There are a variety of different purposes that could be served by such a bulletin board. However, we propose that you set up a bulletin board through which all of the other schools in your district or area can communicate. This BBS can be a vehicle for keeping everyone posted about local news and special school sports events, and for providing important emergency information, such as snow days, to students who have computers at home. As computers become more a part of the home environment, the all-school BBS will be a vehicle for students and schools to communicate with each other.

There are very sophisticated BBS programs that cost several hundred dollars. However, since the requirements of a school BBS are not that demanding, we have chosen a rather inexpensive program that is easy to adapt to individual interests. It is called the ByteMaster BBS. (See Appendix C for ordering information.)

DECIDING ON YOUR MARKET

While you are waiting for your BBS program to arrive (it might take a week or two), be sure to meet together to determine what your audience is to be and what types of information you wish to share. What rules will there be for users? Will users have to join? Will there be time limits for use? Think about the BBSs you have already explored and decide what you like and don't like about them. Will your BBS be open just to all-school users, or will the general public be able to sign on? Make these kinds of decisions now.

WHAT YOU WILL NEED TO KNOW

In order to set up the ByteMaster BBS to meet your own specifications, it is necessary to know some BASIC. For a routine installation, in which you will only be changing PRINT STATEMENTS, very little BASIC is required. If you really want to make substantial changes, however, you will have to be fairly conversant with BASIC.

The instructions that come with the ByteMaster BBS are very complete and quite easy to follow. If you have problems, ask someone with a little more knowledge of computers to help. You can also call the author of the program on his BBS, "The Hospital." Our first try at operating our BBS was not successful, but that was our fault, not the fault of the program or the directions. Difficulties that arise when working with computers are usually the result of human error. Don't be discouraged if it takes several tries before your BBS is operational.

Maintaining the All-School
Bulletin Board

Requires: **Modem**
         BBS

Once the BBS is operational, it will have to be maintained. Messages must be read
and responses made; old notices must be removed and new bulletins added. It
might be a good idea to form a committee to operate the BBS, with a different
member of the group responsible for checking it each day and putting any new
information onto it.

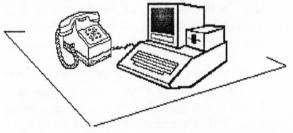

BEING RESPONSIBLE SYSOPS

Although the BBS is mostly fun, it does entail some very specific legal
responsibilities. The most important of these is that you may not allow information
that might cause injury to anyone to remain on your bulletin board. Therefore, you
must check all new messages every day. Information that might cause injury would
include a credit card number of any kind, an unlisted telephone number, computer
access codes and passwords, or private travel plans. The bulletin board exists to
help people, not to cause personal injury, either financial or physical, to anyone.

Since there have now been several legal cases in which sysops have been held
responsible for damage to others, it is important to remind your students that, as
with all things in life, the privilege of operating a bulletin board also involves a
responsibility. If something appears on the BBS that causes concern, the student
should check with an adult. If there is no adult in sight, the message in question
should be removed. The chances are that the students' instincts in these matters will
be reliable, but they should be told to err on the side of caution.

If there is more than one instance of information being placed on your BBS that you feel uncomfortable with, add a message about what is and is not permitted to the instructions to users already on the board. Since you can set up your board so that it can only be used by people whose names, addresses, and account numbers you know, you should quickly be able to find any offending party. By protecting your BBS from abuse, you are also protecting yourself.

Any time your bulletin board cannot be checked daily, such as during school vacations, it should be shut down until a regular schedule can be resumed. Put an announcement on the board so that users will know when to call again.

A GROUP OF SCHOOLS ON THE BOARD

Let's assume that after many discussions, you have decided that every school in your area and every student in each of those schools may have access to your bulletin board. Once the bulletin board has been set up, your school is responsible for its maintenance. Every user can place bulletins, but you, as the sysop, must decide when a message is old and should be removed, as well as whether a message meets your standards of propriety (in other words, no foul language or personal insults allowed).

You must also decide what kinds of announcements can be placed on the bulletin board, and your initial ideas may change as time goes on. You will probably want to include notices about club meetings and sports events, as well as information on a school play or orchestra performance, or a candy sale to raise funds for the Statue of Liberty. You may also want to include a "For Sale" section that would list items--such as a used computer system or a moped--that students want to share with each other.

A student in each school who has a computer at home should be designated as the contact person for the school administration in case of an emergency. This student can then place the information on the bulletin board from home, merely by calling the BBS.

SHOULD THE COMPUTER BE DEDICATED TO THE *BBS*?

The school's computer does not need to be used exclusively for the BBS. Most BBSs work only at night, so the school's computer can be used for other purposes during the school day. However, there should be a regular schedule that all users know. For instance, the BBS might be on from 2:30 in the afternoon until 9:30 in the morning. Maintenance would then take place either from 9:30 to 10:00 each morning, just after shutting down, or from 2:00 to 2:30, just before going back on line.

Your on-line times will be determined by the committee on the basis of what best suits the needs of your users.

Communicating with The Source

Requires: **Modem**
The Source

You have learned to develop data bases for your own personal or school use. However, there are large data bases throughout the country which professional people access on a regular basis. Teachers in need of specialized information call ERIC, which is an educational data base. LEXIS, Westlaw, and ABA Net are data bases for lawyers. Dow Jones is available for investors. NEXIS is a newspaper, magazine, and newsletter service operated by Mead Data Central. Farmers use Agnet, CMN (Computerized Management Network), and Agridata. Photographers can join Photonet or Photo-1. For doctors, there is Minet and BRS Colleague. Newsletter publishers use NewsNet. There is even GameMaster. Dialog is a collection of more than a hundred data bases.

There are also data bases for the general public. Two of these are The Source and CompuServe. Each has news services, an electronic shopping mall, career opportunities, business and financial information, weather forecasts, electronic mail, and facilities for chatting with others on-line. There are games as well as space on the computer to store you own files. You can even make airline reservations through The Source, and do your banking through CompuServe.

SIGNING UP FOR THE SOURCE

To sign up for The Source, call 1-800-336-3366 and say that you are interested in signing up. You will be transferred to an account executive who will ask pertinent information, including the charge account to which you wish your use to be billed.

You will be given an account number, a password, and a local telephone number to call to access The Source, which you will then be able to use immediately.

THE PASSWORD

It is important that students accept the responsibility for maintaining the secrecy of the password. A student who cannot accept this responsibility should not participate in the sharing of it. Using The Source costs money, both for the telephone call and for the cost of the time you are connected to the data base. It is important to use the services in a responsible fashion. If the secrecy of a password is breached, it can be

121

changed immediately by the school administration, either through the system or by telephone. In any case, the teacher in charge should change the password every day.

SIGNING ONTO THE SOURCE

Using your modem program or the procedure outlined in Project 1 of this chapter, dial the local TELENET telephone number provided to the school by The Source. These are local phone numbers that are connected to a national system, which means that you only have to pay the cost of your call to that special number, rather than the charge for a long-distance call to the system's home base.

A sample procedure for connecting with The Source using a local telephone number for the TELENET system is shown below. For other procedures check with the manuals that came with the subscription.

* Using your modem, dial the local phone number for TELENET.
   Your screen shows a prompt (>) and cursor (_) in the upper left-hand corner.
* Press RETURN twice.
   The screen now shows TERMINAL =
* Type **D1** and press RETURN. (**D1** is the identifier for Apples. Other computers require different identifiers. See the manual if necessary.)
   The screen will show the symbol @.
* Type the code given by The Source. It will be an alphanumeric number like **C 30128.** (Remember to leave a space between the C and the number.)
   The computer screen will shortly say:

   30128
   CONNECTED

   WELCOME, YOU ARE NOW
   CONNECTED TO SOURCE SYSTEM 00

   PLEASE TYPE ID
   THEN YOUR
   NUMBER AND PASSWORD
   >

* At the prompt, type **ID,** followed by a space, then your account number, and press RETURN. It should look something like this: **ID   TQ1234.**
* Type your PASSWORD, like **MISTER,** and press RETURN. The password will not appear on the screen.
   The Source will tell you that you are now signed on, give you the last time you were connected, and take you to the ENTRY SCREEN of the MENU.

EXPLORING THE SOURCE

Once you are on-line, select various items from the menu. Go through them and see what kinds of information you can get. If at any time you wish to *break* and go directly to the COMMAND level, hold down the CTRL key and press the letter **P**. It may take a few moments, but you will return to the COMMAND level. The prompt at the COMMAND level looks like this: ==>.

KEY WORDS

The COMMAND level is the entry point into all programs and files on the data base. It is like the front door of a house. From this point on, communicating with The Source is through *key words*. (There is also a menu structure for traveling around The Source, which you may want to explore.) To use the rapid method, you need to know the key word for the part of The Source you want to communicate with.

Using the manual that came with the subscription, select some files that might interest you. Take some time exploring them. Some ideas of files you might try are

MOVIES
UPI
AIRSCHED-D
MUSICSOURCE
POST READ
SKI

When you feel that you are comfortable getting around the system, it will be time to use this powerful new source of information for practical purposes.

If at any time you want to *sign off* from The Source, you have two choices:

1. The neat way to do it is, at the ==> prompt, to type **OFF** followed by pressing RETURN.
2. The not-so-neat way: At any time, turn the computer off. You may be charged for a few minutes that you were actually off-line.

Communicating with CompuServe

Requires: **Modem**
             CompuServe

SIGNING UP FOR COMPUSERVE

To sign up for CompuServe, purchase a Starter Kit from a local computer store. Then, using the CompuServe Network Services phone number listed in the book, call CompuServe with your computer between 6 p.m. and 5 a.m. You will first be asked three questions. Answer them as below:

- After the first question, HOST NAME: type **CIS** (CompuServe Information Service), and press RETURN.
- After the second question, USER ID: type in the ID assigned in your Starter Kit. It is a sequence of numbers like **74166,3054**. Press RETURN.
- After the third question, PASSWORD: type in the password assigned in your Starter Kit. It will look something like this: **DECOY%JUNGLE**. Press RETURN.

      You will then be presented with a menu.

- Select **6** (OTHER) and tell the system how many characters per line and how many lines per page your computer has. With the Apple, indicate **40** characters per line and **24** lines per page.

The computer screen will now show the contract provisions. Read them before agreeing to them. You can get no further into the system until you have agreed to the contract.

After you have agreed to the contract, you will be asked if you wish to sign up permanently. Remember when you sign up that you must also fill in the card in the Starter Kit and mail it in.

You may now use most of CompuServe, although you may not use some of the services, such as EMAIL, until you receive your second password. Nor may you use CompuServe during prime hours. If you need to reach a person at CompuServe, call 1-800-848-8990.

THE PASSWORD

When your school has signed up, paid the initial fee, and arranged for the billing, you are responsible for charges to the school. The concerns regarding password security for accounts with The Source, discussed in Project 4 (see page 120), apply equally to passwords for CompuServe accounts, and the teacher in charge should change the password daily.

SIGNING ONTO COMPUSERVE

From this point on, whenever you sign on to CompuServe, you will be asked for HOST NAME, USER ID, and PASSWORD. When these have been entered, you will see the MAIN MENU.

The prompt for CompuServe is an exclamation point (!).

EXPLORING COMPUSERVE

CompuServe is designed like a book, with the MAIN MENU functioning as the table of contents. The main chapters it lists will include some of the following (CompuServe changes its topics from time to time as it grows to serve its users better):

1. Home Services
2. Business and Financial Services
3. Personal Computing Services
4. Services for Professionals
5. User Information
6. Index

Select the number in front of Home Services, **1**, from the first menu, and press RETURN.

You will now see a new menu. Notice that in the upper left-hand corner it says HOM-1. This is the page number for the menu for Home Services (menus for a service are always on the first page of the chapter). The menu on page HOM-1 gives further choices:

1. Newspapers
2. Weather
3. Reference Library
4. Communications
5. Shop Bank at Home
6. Groups and Clubs
7. Games and Entertainment
8. Education
9. Home Management

You can move through CompuServe either by selecting menu choices or by typing the word **GO** followed by the proper page number at the prompt (!). For instance, the command **GO HOM-10** would send you to page 10 of Home Services. As you work with CompuServe, you will learn the page numbers of your favorite programs and be able to ask for them directly.

Whenever you want to leave the program you are in, hold down the CTRL key and press **P**. CompuServe will return you to the prompt (!). Typing **T** at the prompt will take you to the MAIN MENU, the top. And, typing **M** at the prompt will take you to the previous menu.

When a service requires an additional subscription or additional cost, there will always be a dollar sign ($) preceding or following that choice on the menu.

*   From the Home Services menu, select **2**, Weather.
*   When you have had enough of the weather, break by holding down the CTRL key and pressing **P**.
*   To return to the Home Services menu, type **HOM-1**. Or, return to the MAIN MENU by typing **T** for Top. From this menu, you can then select Home Services. Or, you may go directly to the menu for Games and Entertainment, by typing **GO HOM-60**.

    Choose some games and play to your heart's content. Or almost. Remember that every moment that you are on CompuServe costs money.
*   When you are ready to quit, go to the prompt (!) and type **OFF**.

    You will then be signed off the system.

Chapter 8

Moving On

As today's educators, it is our role to introduce the use of the computer as a valuable tool. We do not have to know everything there is to know about computers. That is not possible. We just have to understand the basic uses of this tool and what it can do, and then pass this understanding on to our students. Let the students decide how it can work for them. Our role is to make the computer available. Then we sit back and relax.

Students today do not need to know how to program computers; they do not need to know BASIC. But they do need to understand what a computer can do, what a valuable tool it is. It is particularly important that they feel comfortable with the technology that has changed the way work is performed. Fortunately, once introduced to a computer's capabilities, they will accept it with joy and no apprehension.

Using computers often makes them better students. From our experience, students who use wordprocessors write better compositions. Students who share data through a data base expand their knowledge. Complex arithmetic is more readily attempted through a spreadsheet. The concepts of graphs are quickly grasped by doing a variety of them with the same data, one right after the other. The programs for art and music available on the market today expand the desire to experiment. And communications, the ability to move information across the telephone lines rapidly--the next great frontier that will soon change the way we live, work, and play--gives students instant access to vast sources of information never previously available to them.

For the revolution to be complete, however, computers must be simple to use, as simple as the telephone. That day is not far away. Learning to use computers has already become far simpler than it used to be: It takes only about 40 minutes to become productive on the Apple Macintosh. These changes are affecting business, too: IBM has come to realize that technical support people at large corporations are dealing with a different group of computer users than they were just a few years ago, a group that demands simplicity, sees the computer as a valuable tool, and wants to use it with as little effort as possible.

To fully understand the impact that microcomputers are having on our society today, it might be useful to imagine, for a moment, what life would be like if a service we take for granted, the United State Post Office, were completely replaced by technological changes.

Parcels are shipped by independent carriers.

Bills are paid by instructing your bank, through a home or office computer, to transfer funds into the accounts of creditors.

You want to thank Aunt Susie for the scarf she sent you for your birthday and bring her up to date on the family. You try the telephone but cannot connect. So you write her a letter on your wordprocessor and then mail it electronically to her through one of a variety of services available to you, through one of the national data bases, or directly to her home computer.

You are browsing through an electronic shopping catalog and want to order that elegant bedspread. With a few keystrokes, the order is placed and the cost is charged to your credit card, or perhaps immediately deducted from your bank account.

Your favorite news magazine is delivered electronically to your home computer by 6 a.m. each Monday morning. You can access it in a variety of ways during the week. You can copy it on to a computer you take with you in the car and listen as the magazine is read to you while you drive to work. Or you can scroll selected articles across your TV screen and read them or have the computer read them to you over breakfast. A special article you want to share with friends can be printed out, copied, and distributed, or, it can be clipped and forwarded electronically.

Is this the future? No, this is the present. All of these capabilities are available-- relatively inexpensively--and in place for people who want to take advantage of them. A world without the post office? Yes, and sooner than you might imagine. Moreover, the services that replace the post office will be easier and cheaper to use.

A very real example of microcomputer technology changing a way of life for an entire nation is taking place in France. The telephone system is moving rapidly toward no longer printing any telephone directories. Instead it plans to provide every telephone user with a small computer that will access an electronic directory for the whole country that will always be up-to-date. This method is seen as cost-effective.

Around the world, access to the equivalent of the printing press is rapidly becoming accessible to more and more people. Guttenberg's invention of movable type revolutionized the use of the written word. Books, pamphlets, and newspapers became possible. Individuals could widely communicate their ideas, for the first time, to people they would never meet. Today, with a computer, a printer, and some software, anyone can create a flyer or a book that looks professionally typeset. For example, with an Apple computer in the classroom and a program called Newsroom, students can create their own newsletters; given access to a copying machine they can share their own ideas with the whole school or with an entire community. This book was prepared for printing using a Macintosh computer, a LaserWriter Printer, and a program called PageMaker, equipment perhaps a bit expensive for a single school, but still under $8,000.

It is the responsibililty of all of our students to make the computer work as an appropriate tool to help meet their goals. Whatever the trade or profession a student of today chooses for the future, an understanding of the use of the computer will be essential. Secretaries type on computers. Truck drivers schedule their trips and determine their loads using computers. Family farmers cannot survive without computerizing many aspects of their operations, including communications with AgriNet, a data base for farmers. Accountants, lawyers, travel agents, shop- keepers, managers within corporations, and assembly-line workers all depend upon computers to get the job done. Inexpensive computer power has revolutionized the way business does business.

We do not know how *your* computer can best be utilized in *your* classroom. We have introduced the major business uses and have attempted to acquaint you with the best software we know on the market today that performs the tasks for which business uses computers: wordprocessing, data base management, spreadsheets, graphing, art and music, and communications. In all cases, the programs are straightforward, easy to use, and inexpensive. We have also given you more than 40 projects in those uses. It is now up to you to use the computer to enhance your own curriculum. Much of what you and your students do can be done-- and improved--using a tool that edits the written word faster, sorts data and graphs it, does complex math easily, and communicates complicated ideas over long distances quickly. With a modest amount of creative planning, you can help your students to incorporate these capabilities in their classwork.

When they learn to use the computer as it was designed to be used, it will become a productivity tool, adaptable to each student's particular needs and enhancing each student's potential.

Appendix A

Using This Book with the IBM PC and PCjr

The Teacher's Computer Book was originally written for the Apple II+ and //e family of computers and was then completely rewritten for the PCjr just before IBM announced that model would be discontinued. Therefore, instead of writing a book for a type of computer that will soon be unavailable, we have included information here for both the IBM PC and the PCjr, making this book as useful for classrooms with IBMs as for those with Apples.

Each of the programs we have used is also available for IBM PCs, except for FlashCalc. We would suggest that for spreadsheets you use VisiCalc (if you have a copy of it) or look for one of the new spreadsheets for IBM PCs that are now available for less than $100. Since the projects we have suggested are not computer specific, nearly all of them will work if you are using IBM computers. In addition, because some BASIC language commands are different for the IBM, we have included another appendix (Appendix B) for pictures and music. The Koala Pad is also available for the IBM, but its menu is slightly different.

The following instructions supplement information in Chapter 1, "Organizing for Computers," which should also be read. When you get to instructions on using the Disk Operating System (DOS) in the section on diskettes, refer to these pages.

USING THE COMPUTER FOR THE FIRST TIME

If you have never used your computer, this is the procedure you should follow every time:

1. Turn on the printer. It has a switch.
2. Turn on the monitor or TV.
3. Place the DOS disk in the drive.
4. Turn the computer on. On the PCjr the switch is in the back, left side. On the PC it is on the right side toward the back.
5. The monitor will show the IBM symbol and the computer will check itself out, counting its internal RAM memory. On the PCjr, the number of K (i.e., thousands of bytes*) of storage available is shown in the lower right-hand

---

* *Byte* is a computer word for "character," like A, M, Z, 1, 6, &, %. Each byte consists of 8 *bits*, or "binary digits," which are 0's and 1's that represent the "off" and "on" states of a switch.

corner of the screen. On the PC, the counting may take place in the upper left-hand corner. (If there is no counting, but the cursor flashes in the upper right-hand corner, the computer is still counting; it is one of the older PCs.)

6. The computer will now ask you to type in the date. You do not have to answer that question. Press the ENTER key.
7. The computer will now ask for the time. Again, just press the ENTER key.
8. The computer will now give you the "A prompt," A>.
9. It is from here that you go into programs or use the DOS commands.

If you are going to be programming in BASIC on the PCjr, follow the same procedures above, but before turning the computer on, place the BASIC cartridge in the left cartridge receptacle and the DOS 2.10 disk in the disk drive. At the A>, type **BASIC** and press the ENTER key.

On the PC, wait until you get the A>, then type **BASICA** (the A is for Advanced BASIC), and press the ENTER key. BASIC is on the DOS disk.

INSTALLING *DOS*

Every program written by an independent software house requires that you *install* DOS on the program disk. That is, you have to copy the disk operating instructions, a program called COMMAND.COM, from the DOS disk onto the new program disk. Every program, at the beginning of its instructions, will tell you how to do this. *Follow these instructions.* They should be very clear. If you have any questions concerning software recommended by this book, call the store from which you purchased the software. If you get no satisfaction, call the software house: Phone numbers are listed in Appendix C.

DOS FUNCTIONS

Formatting a Data Disk Through DOS

If you do not know how to format a data disk through DOS 2.10, the following will be helpful to you. Just follow these steps:

1. Place the DOS disk that came with your computer into the disk drive and turn the computer on.
2. When you are asked for the date and then the time, press the ENTER key. You do not have to answer the questions.
3. At the A>, type **FORMAT**. Press ENTER.
4. Following the computer's instructions, remove the DOS disk from the drive and replace it with a blank disk right out of the box.
5. With the new, blank disk in the drive, press the ENTER key on the keyboard.

The computer will now *format* the disk. It will divide the surface into 40 tracks,

APPENDIX A / 133

each of which is further divided into nine sectors. It will also create a directory for itself so that the computer will be able to find the information you save on it rapidly.

Be sure that all disks are well marked. Write on the label before putting it onto the disk. If you ever have to write on a disk, always use a felt-tipped pen: Ball-point pens and pencils can destroy disks.

Copying Disks

Be sure to make copies of important disks by using the DISKCOPY program on the DOS disk that came with your computer. The following instructions explain the procedure on a system with one disk drive; if your computer has two drives, it will not be necessary to switch disks.

*   At the A>, type **DISKCOPY** and press ENTER.
*   When asked, remove the DOS from the disk drive and place the *source disk,* the one to be copied, into the disk drive.
*   Close the door and press the ENTER key on the keyboard.
*   The drive will whirr. Soon, the computer will ask that you place the *target disk,* the one to be copied to, in the drive. Do so, and press any key.

    The computer will ask you to switch disks every few moments as it copies the programs from the disk.
*   When the computer is finished, it will ask if you wish to make additional copies. Type **Y** or **N**, depending upon whether your choice to make another copy is Yes or No.

Seeing a Directory

Whenever you want to see a listing of files on a disk, use the command **DIR** at the A>. DIR stands for directory.

FINAL THOUGHTS

Beginners on the IBM PC and the PCjr can find help in a number of printed sources. Two books that describe the Disk Operating System in more detail and provide some instruction in BASIC are *The IBM PC: A Beginner's Guide,* and *PCjr: A BASIC Primer,* both by Patricia Shillingburg and both published by Love Publishing Company of Denver.

Appendix B

BASIC on the IBM:
Pictures and Music

Even the youngest children in any school setting can take advantage of the computer's graphics. They only need to learn how to define a graphics screen, select color, plot points, draw lines and circles, and paint.

BOOTING *BASIC*

- Start with the computer off. With the PCjr, place the DOS disk in the disk drive and the BASIC cartridge in the left cartridge drive. You may have to hold the back of the machine to seat the cartridge firmly. With the IBM PC, place the DOS disk in Drive A.
- Turn the computer on.

    You will see an IBM symbol on the blue background (if you have a color monitor or TV). After testing itself, the PCjr may give you an ERROR message in the lower right-hand corner; if it does, ignore the message and press the ENTER key. If there is no ERROR message, or after you have pressed the ENTER key, the disk drive will whirr, the red light will come on, and the computer will start reading information off the disk in the drive.
- When you are asked for the date, press the ENTER key. Do the same when asked for the time. You will now see the A prompt: A>.
- Type **BASIC** (on the PC, type **BASICA**) and press the ENTER key.

    BASIC will come immediately onto the screen. You will see copyright messages on the screen, the expression OK with a blinking bar, and some words across the bottom of the screen. The OK means that the computer is ready to program in BASIC. The blinking bar is called a cursor.

A TOUCH OF *BASIC* GRAPHICS

Defining a Graphics Screen

The PCjr has seven different screens. Six of them are graphics screens, that is, screens for drawing. The PC has only three screens, two of them for graphics. The screen you are going to work with in this project is Screen 1, the medium-resolution screen, which divides the monitor's screen into a grid with 320 pixels, or points, across the screen and 200 pixels down the screen.

- To tell the computer that you wish to use Screen 1, type **SCREEN 1,0**. (The **0** tells the computer that you want to use color.)

    If you make a mistake and the computer does not know what to do with the information you have given it, the computer will print on the screen:

    SYNTAX ERROR
    OK

The computer is saying, "I don't understand. OK, try again."

Introducing Color

Using Screen 1, you may choose a background color from the 16 colors in the computer's spectrum. Each color is assigned a numeric code as follows:

0 Black	4 Red	8 Gray	12 Light Red
1 Blue	5 Magenta	9 Light Blue	13 Light Magenta
2 Green	6 Brown	10 Light Green	14 Yellow
3 Cyan	7 White	11 Light Cyan	15 High-Intensity White

When you select your background color, you may also select a palette of colors to use for drawing. There are two palettes, 0 and 1, and in each palette there are four available colors: the color you have chosen for the background (which is 0 in both palettes) and three others. In Palette 0, 1 is green, 2 is red, and 3 is brown. Characters or letters will appear in yellow. In Palette 1, 1 is cyan, 2 is magenta, and 3 is white. Characters will appear in white.

The color command is: COLOR *background,palette*. For example **COLOR 9,0** means that the background is to be light blue, using the palette of green, red, and brown.

Drawing Lines and Boxes

LINE is a very exciting BASIC statement. With LINE, you can make not only lines, but boxes, and colored-in boxes. The LINE statement is written in the form: LINE *(beginning point)-(ending point),palette color,box fill*.

Using **COLOR 9,0** as above, the statement **LINE(0,0)-(319,199),2** would result in a light blue background with a red line from the upper left-hand corner of the screen to the lower right-hand corner of the screen. **LINE(10,15)-(160,100),1,BF** would put a filled green box on the left to center of the screen. Adding **B** makes a box around a diagonal line. **F** fills it with the selected palette color.

Drawing Circles

The CIRCLE command allows you to draw circles on the screen. The CIRCLE statement is written in the form: CIRCLE *(center point),radius,color*. For example, with the COLOR command written as above (i.e., COLOR 9,0), **CIRCLE (160,100),50,1** would place a large green circle in the middle of the screen.

Coloring Circles

The PAINT command allows you to fill in areas of the screen in color, perhaps inside a circle or a square. The PAINT statement is written in the form: PAINT *(point to begin painting),color to paint,color of boundary*. For instance, to fill in the circle drawn above, type **PAINT (160,100),3,1.** This will give you a brown fill inside the green circle.

Creating a Truck

With just this information, you can create a truck on the computer's screen. Type only the words in bold, and press ENTER after each line. The rest of the line describes what the statement is telling the computer to do.

110 CLS	Clears the Screen
120 SCREEN 1,0	Graphic Color
130 COLOR 1,0	Blue Background, Palette 0
140 LINE (75,75)-(200,150),1,BF	Truck Body
150 LINE (25,100)-(75,150),1,BF	Truck Hood
160 LINE (80,80)-(110,110),3,BF	Truck Window
170 CIRCLE (50,150),25,2	Left Wheel
180 CIRCLE (175,150),25,2	Right Wheel
190 PAINT (50,150),2,2	Paint Left Wheel
200 PAINT (175,150),2,2	Paint Right Wheel

When you have typed this program in, type **RUN** and press ENTER. The computer will run the program.

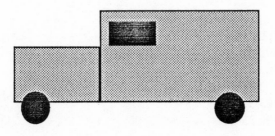

Editing

If it doesn't look like a truck, you will have to look at the program to compare it with the listing above. To see the program, type **LIST** and press ENTER.

Compare the two programs. If you wish to make changes, use the ARROW keys to go to the line that you wish to fix. Make the correction using the INSERT or DELETE keys. Use the RIGHT ARROW key to go to the end of the line and then press ENTER.

Use the DOWN ARROW key to go beyond the end of the program and then press ENTER. Now, RUN the program again.

Saving

To save your program, place a formatted data disk in the drive. Then type **SAVE"TRUCK** (no spaces) and press ENTER.

MAKING MUSIC WITH *BASIC*

By learning just a few BASIC statements, you can make music on your IBM PC or PCjr.

The computer has its own speaker, but the sound is a bit tinny. You can improve the sound by hooking the computer up to a television, which has its own speaker, or to an independent speaker.

Sound

The sounds we hear have two characteristics: frequency and duration. Frequency determines the pitch of a sound. Low-pitch sounds have lower frequencies and high-pitch sounds have higher ones. A low sound may have a frequency of 37 vibrations per second, and a high-pitch sound may have a frequency of 20,000 vibrations per second.

To make sound on the computer, we must tell the computer how many vibrations per second we want a note to have and how long it is to play that sound.

The SOUND statement is written in the form: SOUND *frequency, duration.* Frequency must be in the range of 37 to 32767, 37 being the lowest note and 32767 the highest. Duration must be between 0 and 65535, with each whole number representing approximately one-eighteenth (1/18) of a second. Try these sounds:

```
SOUND 37,25
SOUND 100,35
SOUND 250,45
SOUND 400,50
SOUND 700,45
SOUND 1000,35
```

Middle C has a frequency of 262. The BASIC manual that came with your computer lists all of the different frequencies for notes one octave below and three octaves above middle C.

Creating Loops

In computer programming, *loops* are a means of telling the computer to repeat a set of commands a specified number of times, making it unnecessary to type in those commands each time you want them executed. Loops are created with a FOR-NEXT statement in the form: FOR *variable = initial value* TO *end value* followed by the commands you want repeated, followed by the statement NEXT *variable*. The *variable* is an identifier that tells the computer which FOR and NEXT go together; since you can program loops within loops, it is important to know which FOR relates to which NEXT. The FOR-NEXT statement is a common BASIC command; it is not peculiar to graphics or music. Nor is it peculiar to the IBM BASIC.

Using Loops: Adding Sound to the Truck

The truck you made in the last chapter is rather silent. Let's give it a horn.

- Place the disk that has the truck saved onto it into the drive. Type
  LOAD"TRUCK (no spaces) and press ENTER.
- To LIST the program, type LIST and press ENTER.
    The truck program is now on the screen.
- Add these lines:

```
210 FOR S = 1 TO 10
220 SOUND 100,5
230 SOUND 250,5
240 NEXT S
```

These statements tell the computer to make two different sounds and to repeat them, one after the other, ten times. Notice that we have used "S" as the variable that links the FOR statement with the NEXT statement.

- Now RUN the truck program again. How do you like that?
- Save the new TRUCK program. It will write over the old TRUCK program on the disk if you call it just TRUCK. But to keep both of them, just call it something else, like TRUCK2. So type SAVE"TRUCK2 (no spaces) and press ENTER.

Using PLAY

The statement PLAY allows you to write a program using the letter names of notes, such as A, B, C, D, as we call them when writing music for musical instruments.

These are some things you need to know before you begin.

The letters are placed between quotation marks.
The computer keyboard has seven octaves (0-6). Octave 3 begins with middle
    C. Unless you choose another, the computer will select octave 4.
Length (L) tells the computer how long the note is to play. L1 = whole note,
    L2 = half note, L4 = quarter note, and so forth.

Here is a program that uses these ideas in PLAY.

Mary Had a Little Lamb

```
100 CLS
120 SCREEN 1,0
130 PRINT "MARY HAD A LITTLE LAMB"
140 PLAY "o3L4EDCDEEL2E"
150 PLAY "L4DDL2DL4EGL2GL4EDCDEEEEDDEDL1C"
160 END
```

Now RUN the program.
When you are satisfied, SAVE the program as MARY. Type **SAVE"MARY**
(no spaces) and press ENTER.

Your Turn

Now that you have learned how to use COLOR, LINE, CIRCLE, PAINT,
SOUND, PLAY, and FOR-NEXT, it is time for you to write your own graphics
programs. Be sure to look the statements up in the BASIC manual that came with
your IBM to learn more about them.

Appendix C
Useful Addresses

Bank Street Writer

> **Broderbund Software**
> 17 Paul Drive
> San Rafael, California 94903
> 415-479-1170

> **Scholastic, Inc.**
> 2931 E. McCarty Street
> P.O. Box 7502
> Jefferson City, Missouri 65102
> 800-325-6149

PFS File, Report, Graph

> **Software Publishing Company**
> 1901 Landings Drive
> Mountain View, California 94043
> 415-962-8910

FlashCalc

> **Paladin**
> 2700 Augustine Drive - Suite 178
> Santa Clara, California 95054
> 408-970-0566

Koala Pad

> **Koala Products, PTI Industries**
> 269 Mount Hermon Road
> Scotts Valley, California 95066
> 408-438-0946

Songwriter

Mindscape, Inc.
3444 Dundee Road
Northbrook, Illinois 60062
800-221-9884

Hayes Modem

Hayes Micro Computer Products, Inc.
5932 Peachtree Industrial Blvd.
Norcross, Georgia 30092
404-449-8791

ByteMaster BBS

To get a copy of ByteMaster BBS (BMBBS), send a check for $49.95, plus $2.00 for shipping and handling to:

ByteMaster Software
P.O. Box 366
Livingston, New Jersey 07039

You must give the following information:

Your name and address
The phone number and address of your BBS
The type of modem you will be using
Whether you want the Apple or the IBM version

Remember, this is a copyrighted program and can only be used for the designated BBS.

CompuServe

CompuServe, Inc.
5000 Arlington Center Blvd.
Columbus, Ohio 43220
614-457-8600

The Source

The Source
1616 Anderson Road
McLean, Virginia 22101
703-734-7500

About the Authors

PATRICIA MOSER SHILLINGBURG is a management computer education consultant. She develops and implements software training programs for IBM, Hewlett Packard, Wang, and Apple microcomputer systems. Previous books include *Kids Can Touch Computers, Adults Can Touch Computers, The IBM PC: A Beginner's Guide,* and *IBM PCjr: First Steps in BASIC Programming,* all published by Love Publishing Company, Denver, Colorado. She is an active advocate for the mentally retarded and is the founder of Our House, Inc., which provides group home programs in the greater Summit, New Jersey, area. She received her B.A. from Wheaton College in Massachusetts.

KENNETH CRAIG BAREFORD has been an elementary school teacher since 1967. He received his B.S. degree from Lehigh University and his M.A. from Kean College of New Jersey. He introduced computers into the "gifted and talented" program in the Summit (New Jersey) Public School District in 1983 and currently encourages "publishing" and communications with his students. He was a member of the team that wrote and implemented the computer curriculum for his district and has taught computer literacy at Kean College. For three years, he was the producer of MicroTalk, a computer education program on TV36, the local access channel.

JOYCE ANN PACIGA has a B.A. from Kean College and an M.A. from Rutgers University. She has been a classroom teacher for 13 years in the Summit (New Jersey) School District. She pioneered the use of microcomputers in her district in 1979 and worked on the development and implementation of the computer curriculum for her system. She also has experience teaching computer programming at Summit Micro and in private schools. Joyce is currently vice president of the Suburban Council of the International Reading Association and received a teaching excellence award as part of Governor Kean's Teacher Recognition Program.

JANIS LUBAWSKY TOWNSEND, Ph.D., earned her doctorate in English from Wayne State University with a dissertation on Gertrude Stein. Experience writing with a wordprocessor led her to develop a college-level writing program using a mainframe text editor. Currently, she is a consultant to corporations and educators on course design in PC and Apple software training, writes manuals for software products, and leads training programs.

The Teacher's Computer Book: 40 Student Projects to Use with Your Classroom Software was written on an Apple Macintosh computer using MacWrite. Page layout was completed using PageMaker, by the Aldus Corporation, and the Apple LaserWriter printer. Charts, graphs, and spreadsheets where created using MacDraft. Sources for artwork include ClickArt by T/Maker Graphics, Springboard's Art a la Mac, and The Mac Art Dept., by Tom Christopher.